Data Analysis in Hotel and Catering Management

Data Analysis in Hotel and Catering Management

Stephen Cunningham

Butterworth-Heinemann Ltd
Linacre House, Jordan Hill, Oxford OX2 8DP

 PART OF REED INTERNATIONAL BOOKS

OXFORD   LONDON   BOSTON
MUNICH   NEW DELHI   SINGAPORE   SYDNEY
TOKYO   TORONTO   WELLINGTON

First published 1991

British Library Cataloguing in Publication Data
Cunningham, Stephen
    Data analysis in hotel and catering management.
    I. Title
    647.9

ISBN 0 7506 0111 6

Printed and bound in Great Britain by Billings & Sons, Worcester

Contents

Preface

This book is based on a series of lectures given at Portsmouth Polytechnic over the period 1980 to 1987 to first-year students taking a BA or HND in Hotel and Catering Management. In the beginning the emphasis of the course was on the methods used in quantitative analysis but successive groups of customers quickly made it clear that it was the applications that interested them. At the same time, they became aware that, generally though not always, more realistic applications do not have simple solutions. The result is a compromise that is intended to provide an understanding of the methods and give an indication of their scope of application, without becoming submerged by the inevitable detail of a real problem. Other applications will become apparent either as the course of study being followed proceeds or once some experience of the industry is gained.

As the references given in this book show, there is increasing interest in the application of quantitative methods in the hotel and catering industry. This trend seems bound to continue and it is hoped that this book will provide readers with the basic knowledge required to appreciate the methods used and the results obtained (in particular, to understand the limitations of the methods and the validity of the results).

As is usual many people played a role in the development of this book. While it is always invidious to select some individuals at the expense of others, I must thank (without implicating) Gerry Banks of Highbury College of Technology and, particularly, Eric Woolley of Portsmouth Polytechnic, for their advice and encouragement when this project was in its formative stage.

Finally, I must thank my family for their support and encouragement when time was in short supply to finish this book among many other commitments. I hope it was all worth while.

Stephen Cunningham

1
Introduction

The purpose of this book is to demonstrate how to analyse, using statistical methods, the kind of data likely to be available to managers in the hotel and catering industry and how to interpret the results of such analysis. The examples and applications that are used to illustrate the basic methods are almost always directly applicable to management situations. So far as is possible, traditional statistics examples involving coloured balls, card games and so on have been avoided. Sometimes, however, the use of such examples greatly facilitates explanation and in these cases they have been retained.

The emphasis of the book is on the methods of analysis rather than on the applications. It is the methods that are general, and by the end of this book the reader will be able to apply them to a much wider range of problems than it is possible to discuss in a single book. Apart from the examples developed in the text, further possible applications are indicated in the exercises which accompany different chapters.

The book is intended to be self-contained. It should be accessible even to readers whose mathematics is a little rusty, particularly if they have some familiarity with computers, via for instance the use of spreadsheets or database maintenance. No formal proofs of results are presented here. The book concentrates rather on the utilization of these results. Moreover, relatively little attention is given to number-crunching methods since it is assumed that most readers will have access to a computer. Few calculations deriving from statistical methods are particularly complex and most can be quite easily handled using a computer spreadsheet. In addition, tables exist presenting the results of, for example, probability calculations using the most common probability distributions. The tables referred to throughout this book are those compiled by Murdoch and Barnes (1970) but many other equally useful compilations exist. The combination of such tables and microcomputers means that statistics no longer comprises tedious exercises in numerical calculation. Rather attention centres, as in this book, on method and interpretation.

Computers and statistics

The development of microcomputers has brought computing within most people's reach. However, while computing offers quick and simple solutions to many tedious problems, it also requires an ongoing investment of time to master and maintain the basic elements.

A basic computer literacy seems to require some knowledge of the following elements:

1 The basic operating environment of your computer (MS-DOS or other operating system). The computing used in this book was done using MS-DOS on IBM-compatible microcomputers.
2 Programming (at least at an elementary level). Some chapters contain listings of computer programs. These are all written in BASIC which seems to be the most widely-understood language.
3 A word-processing package (such as Word Perfect).
4 A spreadsheet package (such as Lotus 123).
5 A database package (such as DBase).
6 A graphics package (such as Freelance used for the graphs in this book).
7 A statistical package (such as SPSS).

Some integrated software packages are available (e.g. Symphony from Lotus) which provide the first three or four functions. As is to be expected, the limits of such packages are reached more quickly than is the case with software specializing in one application. Whether it is worth learning three or more packages depends on the use to which you are going to put them. If you are going to limit yourself to small-scale applications then an integrated package is probably the best bet. On the other hand, if you are going to analyse a large-scale database, even the specialized packages mentioned above may become inadequate and you may have to move to a larger machine.

If you do not invest sufficient time in training then you will end up wasting time looking through manuals trying to find ways of doing particular tasks. In addition, most off-the-shelf packages are becoming increasingly complex (see for example DBase IV) so that it is often difficult to find out, let alone master, all the functions of which they are capable. The knowledge of at least one fundamental programming language (BASIC, Pascal, C, etc.) is increasingly necessary since the packages themselves are often programmable. If you have no knowledge of programming concepts then you will certainly not maximize the benefits to be derived from packages.

As the book proceeds, computer-based approaches are developed wherever possible. Such approaches are limited, however, to an illustration of the techniques. This is a book about data analysis, not about computing. The most difficult part of a computer package, especially a statistics one such as SPSS, is interpreting the output that is produced. It is on this aspect that the book concentrates.

Some definitions

In this section, we shall introduce and define some of the more important concepts in statistics. This will serve also to introduce the plan of the book and to indicate the topics discussed in each chapter.

Statistical methods are generally broken into two parts – descriptive and inferential. *Descriptive statistics* comprises the set of methods, both pictorial and numerical, that may be used to describe a data set. These methods are discussed in Chapters 2 and 3. Their main purpose is to provide the reader with a clear and accurate summary of a large and/or complex data set. This function is extremely important. If the data description is poorly done, then a misleading impression of the data set can easily be given. Moreover, statistics is a subject where each element builds on a previous one. The fundamental element is the data description. If this is flawed then so also will be the subsequent data analysis based upon it.

Inferential statistics is that part of statistics that is of most use in business decision-making. Here we take a sample from a statistical population and use the sample to make inferences about the population. Since information is necessarily incomplete (the sample being smaller than the population), such situations are uncertain. Once a situation is uncertain, the best that can be done from a decision-making viewpoint is to calculate how likely are particular results. This calculation is done on the basis of *probability*. Chapters 4, 6 and 7 consider the ideas underlying probability, and Chapters 8, 9, 10 and 11 apply them to particular situations.

In practice, the use of sampling is very hard to avoid. Consider for instance a company carrying out a market research study. The purpose of the research is to enable the company to know its customers better. However, it is quite obvious that unless the company is unusually specialized, it will be too expensive to contact all potential customers (this being the population in this case). The company is forced therefore to choose a sample of customers whose opinions, it hopes, are representative of all customers. If the sample is *biased* (i.e. it is not representative) in some way then conclusions drawn from its analysis may induce costly policy errors. The problem of how to choose a representative sample is a difficult, but crucially important, one. It is discussed in detail in Chapter 5.

The term *statistical population* is used above in connection with people. In business situations, statistical populations often do involve people but it is important to note that in statistics the term is perfectly general. It need have nothing to do with people and refers merely to the complete set of items being studied. If, for example, you are studying the weight of tinned goods packed by a machine, then the statistical population will be all tins produced during the study period.

A population may be *infinite* (or effectively so) – for example, all potential guests at a hotel during a year – or *finite* – for example, all actual guests at a hotel during a year. Sampling from a finite population complicates probability calculations. However, any population can effectively be made infinite if sampling is done *with replacement*. That is, the selected item is noted and then returned to the population so that it may be chosen again.

Another important issue in sampling concerns the size of the sample that must be taken if accurate results are to be obtained. Two approaches are possible. First, where very small samples cannot be avoided (for example, because of cost), specially designed probability methods – notably the *t*-distribution – should be used. This distribution is discussed in Chapter 9. Second, in the situation where we can choose the size of the sample, we can define a maximum error that we are prepared to tolerate in our results and then calculate the sample size required to meet this. This method is discussed in Chapter 10.

Finally, the *data* being studied may be categorized in a number of ways. To begin with, we can distinguish between *cross-section* and *time-series* data. The former refers to a situation where we have data concerning a variable at a given point in time – for example, the price charged today by the ten different hotels in a town. Time-series data refers to a situation where we have data on a given variable over a period of time – for example, the daily price charged by hotel A over a year. Much data available in business tends to be of a time-series nature. Such data are especially useful for forecasting purposes (see Chapter 12).

We can also distinguish between *discrete* and *continuous* data. A discrete data set is one where the variable under consideration may only have certain, specific values. An example would be the guest. It is not possible for 0.235 of a guest to appear at the hotel and hence the number of guests increases in units of one. A continuous variable on the other hand is one that may take on any value subject only to the accuracy of the measuring device. Examples include time and height. You, for instance, must have had at some point every conceivable height between your height at birth and that which you have now. Due to measurement problems, you probably never gave your height as 65.21458914 centimetres but at some point you must have measured this.

The difference between discrete and continuous variables is of some importance. It is much easier mathematically to analyse continuous variables and for this reason much of statistics has been developed assuming that the data set refers to such a variable. In business however almost all variables are discrete. Care must therefore be taken in the application of statistical methods since frequently a continuous distribution must be used to approximate a discrete one. Fortunately, in most situations discrete data can be organized so that the approximation is valid.

A note on notation

Those who are new to statistics are often put off to find Greek letters spread liberally through the text. However, the use of the Greek alphabet is extremely useful since it enables a clear and simple distinction to be made between the population and the sample. Concepts relating to the sample are generally abbreviated using Roman letters, whereas those relating to the population are abbreviated using Greek letters. By and large the same letter is used in each case – for example, the sample standard deviation is denoted by s and the population standard deviation by the Greek s, σ (called sigma). An important exception to this rule concerns the mean – the sample mean is denoted as $\bar{x}$ whereas the population mean is denoted by the Greek m, μ (pronounced mew). Note also that the difference between lower and upper case Greek letters is important. The upper case Greek s, Σ, denotes the sum of a series of numbers. The really important thing to note however is that the symbols in themselves have no meaning. They are simply a shorthand way of expressing concepts so that instead of having to write, for instance, population mean each time we refer to it, we have merely have to write μ. Do not be over-impressed therefore by the use of such symbols.

Having considered a number of important introductory issues, we will now turn our attention to the problem of descriptive statistics. The description of data using graphical and numerical methods is discussed in the following two chapters.

Reference

MURDOCH, J. and BARNES, J. (1970), *Statistical Tables*, 2nd edn, Macmillan.

2
The organization and graphical presentation of data

Statistics is principally concerned with the collection and analysis of numerical data. In many cases the amount of information collected is so large that it is difficult to make much sense of it unless it is organized in some way. This organization of data is one of the most basic and important elements of statistics since it paves the way for both a graphical presentation of the situation and any analysis that may be needed. In this chapter we shall look first at the way in which data sets may be classified to make them more easily understood. We shall then look at some pictorial methods that may be used to represent the data. In the next chapter we shall consider the main numerical methods that may be used to summarize data sets.

Data classification

Probably the easiest way to proceed is to consider an example. Suppose that during a particular week a hotel surveys 65 of its guests. This survey reveals various facts about the guests one of which is that their (declared) ages, to the nearest whole year, are as shown in Table 2.1.

Table 2.1 *The ages of guests (to nearest whole year)*

32	36	39	42	58	46	37	41	41	52
3	1	27	25	41	52	55	45	39	40
16	75	63	38	22	34	23	48	50	19
27	45	12	70	62	35	31	49	57	61
35	17	39	47	78	28	37	41	59	40
34	41	32	62	55	12	45	28	27	31
70	56	33	38	44					

Source: hypothetical data

In this form it is very difficult to make much of the data and imagine how much worse the problem would have been with 650 guests rather than 65. Our objective is to organize the data so as to present an accurate but more readily comprehensible picture of the situation. The first step is to classify the data.

Students are sometimes put off by the fact that *within limits* there is not really a right answer to this kind of exercise. At some point each individual must make up his or her own mind as to how best to proceed. There is nonetheless a set of guidelines to follow in the classification of any data set. These guidelines are:

1   The number of classes must be a compromise between too much detail and too little. Depending on the number of observations (i.e. values), the number of classes might vary between 5 and 20.

2   When establishing the classes the *class boundaries* must clearly separate one class from the next, otherwise it will not be obvious into which class the observations should be placed. For instance, suppose in the case of the data set in Table 2.1 we had a class going from 18-28 and another from 28-38. There is one observation of 28 and with these class boundaries it is not clear whether it should go in the first or the second class. It may even end up being counted twice. One way to ensure that classes remain separate is to make the boundary slightly more accurate than any of the data. In the above example, all the data are in whole years. If therefore we denominate our boundaries in terms of half-years there is no danger of the boundary coinciding with an actual data point. For example, if we have a class from 18.5-28.5 and another from 28.5-38.5 it is now quite clear that the value of 28 should be placed into the first class. An alternative method of classification which is often used has classes such as 18 to less than 28, 28 to less than 38 and so on. Here again it is clear into which class the observation 28 should be placed.

3   Once a data point has been placed into the appropriate class, its individual value is lost. We simply know that it must have a value lying between the class boundaries. To overcome this problem the class mid-point or *class mark* is taken to represent all the values in the class. In other words it is assumed that they all have this same value regardless of their real value. This amounts to assuming that the values are evenly spread through the class and that the centre value is therefore representative. This may not always be so, especially with end-classes, and is one cost of classifying the data.

4   Classes do not have to be all of the same width. In fact, with many data sets it is impossible to provide a good representation without using different class widths.

5   Finally a little jargon: the *class frequency* is the number of observations in a particular class. The *total frequency* is then just the sum of

the class frequencies which should be the same as the total number of observations (i.e. 65 in the above example) if the classification has been carried out correctly.

Bearing these general rules in mind, let us now classify the data on ages. First, we must decide how many classes to have. As there are only 65 observations, it would clearly be nonsense to have 20 classes since each class would have too few values for any meaningful picture to emerge. Looking at the data set there seem to be few values below 20 and above 60, and these values may therefore be used to establish classes at the low and high end of the data set. Most of the observations are in the middle age range and a narrower classification is required here. The six classes shown in column 1 of Table 2.2 seem to provide a reasonable compromise.

Having decided upon the class boundaries, we must next organize the data into the separate classes. For this we require a second column called the *tally*. Here we consider each observation in turn and note the class in which it lies. We may then calculate the class frequencies as in column 3 of Table 2.2 The set of class frequencies is called the *frequency distribution*.

Table 2.2   *Classifying the data on the age of guests*

1 Class Boundaries	2 Tally	3 Class Freqs (f)	4 Relative Class Freqs (f/n) × 100%
less than 20	11111 11	7	10.8
20 – less than 30	11111 111	8	12.3
30 – less than 40	11111 11111 11111 11	17	26.2
40 – less than 50	11111 11111 11111 1	16	24.6
50 – less than 60	11111 1111	9	13.8
60 and over	11111 111	8	12.3
	Total $= n =$ 65		100.0

Source: Table 2.1

Now that the data are classified it becomes clearer that, while there is a reasonable spread of ages, the hotel is attracting customers principally in the 30 to 50 age group, at least during the period when this sample was taken. This may have certain implications for the management of the hotel either in terms of improving the facilities for this age range or in making the hotel more attractive to those age ranges presently under-represented.

The calculation and presentation of the frequency distribution is clearly very useful since it clarifies the interpretation of the data. If, however, we are interested in comparing two or more samples or populations of different sizes then it may be more appropriate to consider the *relative frequency distribution*. This latter simply tells you the proportion (or percentage) of observations that are in each class. Hence relative class frequency is found by dividing class frequency by total frequency and then multiplying by 100 if a percentage answer is desired. The relative frequency distribution of our age data is shown as column 4 of Table 2.2.

Although it is very helpful to present data numerically, from the point of view of pure data presentation a better impact may generally be achieved visually. Let us go on therefore to consider pictorial methods of data presentation.

Data as pictures

The histogram

Probably the best known of the visual data presentation methods is the histogram. This comprises a series of rectangles or bars with the following characteristics. Each bar has its base on the horizontal axis and is drawn so as to be centred on the class mark. It has a width equal to that of the class and hence not all bars need have the same width. It is important to note that a natural (normal) scale continues to be used on the horizontal axis even if the classes are of differing widths. It is not acceptable to draw all classes the same and then to write underneath, for example, 10-15 15-25. This is because the visual impression created by such a method is inaccurate.

The most important characteristic of a histogram, however, is that it is the *area* (and not the height!) of each bar that represents the number of observations in the class. This is without doubt the most common error made in drawing histograms. It presumably arises because many people initially learn to draw histograms where the class widths are all the same. In this special case the area of each bar depends only on its height. Nonetheless it is the area and not the height which is important. This is well demonstrated by a version of a diagram presented in Yeomans (1968, p. 72) and redrawn here as Figure 2.1. Let us suppose that the turnover of hotel A is twice as much as that of hotel B. We may show this correctly by drawing two vertical lines one of which is twice as long as the other. The eye now sees the truth.

Suppose, however, that we give the diagram some area by completing the square. Although the height of square A is only twice that of square B, each side of the former is twice that of the latter with the result that the *area* of A is four times that of B rather than the twice that we are supposed to be showing. The situation becomes even worse if we use an object, such as a money-bag (still with the same height), since we must now

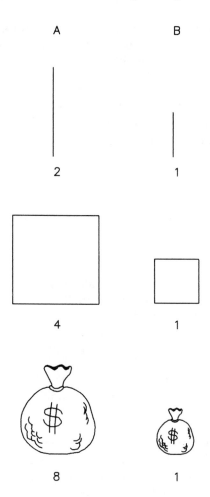

Figure 2.1   *Visual impact of area and volume*

contend with volume. The result now is that the visual impression says A is eight times greater than B. Sometimes this kind of mistake is made inadvertently but, as Darrell Huff's book *How to Lie with Statistics* makes clear, often the intention is deliberately to deceive.

Where the class widths are not the same, the heights of the classes must be adjusted appropriately so that the area provides an accurate picture. However before we can do this in our example we must first address another issue which is what to do in the case of open-ended classes – i.e. less than 20, and 60 and over. The only way that classes such as these may be given a finite area is to close them arbitrarily at some value. If this is not done we have no way of knowing how high they should be drawn.

Once again there is no one right way of doing this but the cardinal rule is that the values chosen to close the classes should make sense in the context of the rest of the histogram.

In the case of the 'less than 20' class the choice of where to close the class is obvious; clearly no one can have an age less than zero and so this value may be taken. In the case of the upper class (60 and over) the decision is less clear-cut. The class before this (50 to less than 60) has a width of ten years so it would not make sense to make the final class narrower than this. On the other hand too high a value would conflict with the medical evidence regarding longevity. For our purposes a value of 80 would seem to be a reasonable compromise.

Now that the two open-ended classes have been (arbitrarily) closed we may proceed to draw the histogram. It should be noted, however, that this is not the only reason for closing classes. Unless this is done it is impossible to establish class marks (class mid-points) and it is these that serve as the basis for all numerical work, such as calculating averages. Table 2.3 summarizes the above discussion and shows the class marks.

Table 2.3   *The classification of the data on the age of guests*

1 Class boundaries	2 Class widths	3 Class mark	4 Frequency
0 – less than 20	20	10	7
20 – less than 30	10	25	8
30 – less than 40	10	35	17
40 – less than 50	10	45	16
50 – less than 60	10	55	9
60 – less than 80	20	70	8
			—
			Total 65

Source: Table 2.1

In drawing the histogram the easiest way to adjust the heights so as to make the area represent frequency is to choose one class as the base class. The heights of all other classes should then be adjusted to this. It makes no difference which class is taken as the base provided, of course, that the adjustment is correctly carried out. As a general rule less work will be required if the most commonly occurring class width is taken as the base. In the example here this would mean taking a base width of ten years. The heights of the remaining classes may then be related to the base class using one simple formula:

$$\text{Height} = \text{Class frequency} \times \frac{\text{Base class width}}{\text{Actual class width}}$$

In Table 2.3 there are only two classes that are not standard – the first and the last. Both of these have widths of twenty years. Applying the above formula to these classes gives the following results:

$$\text{Height of first class} = 9 \times \frac{10}{20} = 4.5$$

$$\text{Height of last class} = 7 \times \frac{10}{20} = 3.5$$

In both cases it is apparent that as the class is twice as wide as the base class the height must be halved.

The histogram may now be drawn and this is shown as Figure 2.2. This histogram is correctly drawn with the heights adjusted so that the area of the bars represents the frequencies of the classes and an accurate visual impression of the data set is thereby given. The objective that we established at the beginning is now achieved. The data have been organized and presented so as to be comprehensible to the reader at a glance without accuracy being sacrificed.

The histogram is a summary presentation of our original data set. The histogram in its turn may also be summarized! This is done in one of two ways. First, we may draw the *frequency polygon* which is a set of straight lines connecting class mid-point to class mid-point at the top of each bar. It is customary to complete the polygon by bringing it down to the X-axis at each end, as is shown in Figure 2.2. The second method of summarizing the histogram is via the *frequency curve*. In Figure 2.2 what seems to be the most appropriate curve has been superimposed. The advantage of such a curve is that the most appropriate one may be found, as we shall see in later chapters, using mathematical techniques. Although they may be difficult to prove, these techniques are simple to apply; and we do not even need to draw the histogram to do so. Hence a good visual description of most data sets may be found fairly easily. When we come to study frequency curves in detail later, keep in mind that they are nothing more complicated than summaries of histograms.

Cumulative frequency and the ogive

In some situations it may be of particular interest to see the way in which the data set builds up. We can do this by establishing what is called the

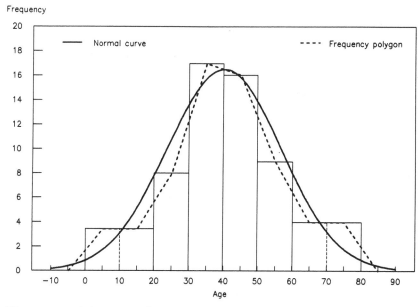

Figure 2.2   *Histogram of age data presented in Table 2.1*

cumulative frequency and drawing its graph which is called the ogive. There are two possible cumulative frequency distributions that may be derived for each data set. These are called 'less than' cumulative frequency and 'more than' cumulative frequency. They are most easily explained by continuing the example begun above, and Table 2.4 shows the two cumulative frequencies calculated for our age data. To understand how they were calculated, let us consider the 'less than' cumulative frequency (c.f.) first.

Table 2.4   *Cumulative frequency of the data on the ages of guests*

Class boundaries	Class frequencies	Less than c.f.	More than c.f.
-20 to less than 0	0	0	65
0 to less than 20	7	7	58
20 to less than 30	8	15	50
30 to less than 40	17	32	33
40 to less than 50	16	48	17
50 to less than 60	9	57	8
60 to less than 80	8	65	0
	65		

Source: Table 2.1

Less than the age of zero there is obviously no one so this gives us our starting point. Less than age 20 there are 9 observations. Less than age 30 there are 15 observations – 6 in the 20–30 class and 9 in the 0–20 class. Less than age 40 there are 24 observations (9 + 6 + 9), and so on. In this way the less than cumulative frequency is established and we can see the way in which the data set builds up according to age. Figure 2.3 shows the 'less than' ogive which gives the visual impression of the data set build up.

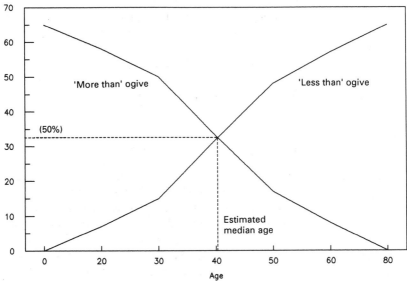

Figure 2.3   *The ogive*

The 'more than' c.f. may be calculated in a similar manner, except that everything is reversed. Hence every one has an age greater than zero and so the 'more than' c.f. is 50. Only 41 people however have an age more than 20 (50 minus the 9 aged between 0 and 20), and only 35 exceed 30 years of age. The remaining values are calculated similarly. The 'more than' ogive is also shown in Figure 2.3.

The alert reader may have noticed that there is a small problem with the 'more than' c.f. as it has been calculated here. This is that the value 20 is included in the class 20 to less than 30. Hence strictly speaking we should say 20 or more, rather than more than 20. This makes no real difference, but the sticklers for accuracy might prefer to call it the 'more than or equal to' c.f.

Notice that to simplify calculation we add an empty class at the beginning of the table (−20 to 0). This class is useful since it enables us to bring both ogives to the horizontal axis. Note also that the method of calculating the cumulative frequency shown here enables a simple check for accuracy to be made because the sum of the 'less' and 'more than' cumulative frequencies at each level should equal the total frequency. For instance, taking the class 0–less than 20 we have a 'less than' c.f. of 11 and 'more than' (or equal to) of 54 giving a total of 65.

The ogives in Figure 2.3 have the typical elongated-S shape. Notice that the two curves intersect at 50% of the cumulative frequency – that is they divide the data set into two equal halves. The value corresponding to this on the horixontal axis is called the *median* which here is approximately 41 years. In other words 50% of the people in the sample are more than 41 years old and 50% less. We shall consider the median in more detail in the next chapter.

In the same way that we calculated the relative frequency associated with the frequency distribution, we may calculate the relative cumulative frequency distribution. As before the main use of this is for comparison of different sets of results.

Time-series data and their graphical presentation

The data that we have considered so far regarding the ages of guests clearly relate to a particular point in time. This kind of data is called *cross-section*. However, many of the data sets of interest in hotel and catering management are *time-series*. That is to say they represent observations of the same variable at different points in time. An example might be the profit performance of a hotel over a specific period. The graphing of time-series data raises one or two particular problems.

A first problem is how should we graph series that show little change? The answer depends on what the graphical presentation is intended to achieve. So far the objective has been to present an accurate picture of the complete data set and if this remains our goal then the graph should be complete. If however the purpose is to highlight some particular aspect of the data then an incomplete graphical presentation *may* be more appropriate. To clarify what is meant by this let us consider an example.

The data in Table 2.5 relate to employment in the hotel and catering industry over the period 1980 to 1982. Figure 2.4 shows a graph of these data. The graph is complete in the sense that the vertical axis has been drawn to scale. The result is that the reader can see that employment changed little over the period although its level did fluctuate. This is the correct interpretation of events. However, it may also be noticed that the fluctuations in employment are related to the time of the year. Let us suppose that our aim is to highlight these fluctuations. In this case Figure 2.5 is more appropriate. Here the vertical axis has been truncated with the clear result that the changes in employment are emphasized.

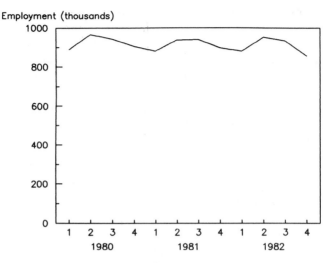

Figure 2.4   *Employment in the UK hotel and catering industry*

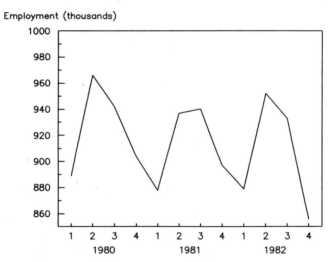

Figure 2.5   *Employment with truncated vertical axis*

It must be noted however that Figure 2.5 would be totally inappropriate to display the level of employment. It would give the misleading
impression that employment had been, relatively, very variable; this
would be true even if the actual data is put onto the vertical axis. Even if
one is told by the numbers that the data set does not change much, the
visual impression will remain that it does. Those people who wish to use

Table 2.5 *Employment in the hotel and catering industry in the UK*

Year	Quarter	Employment (thousands)
1980	1	889
	2	966
	3	942 (estimated)
	4	904
1981	1	878
	2	937
	3	940
	4	897
1982	1	879
	2	952
	3	933
	4	856

Source: *Department of Employment Gazette*, February 1984

statistics to mislead tend to make great use of this fact. Some may even decide to give you no help by leaving out the numbers. What interpretation would you put on Figure 2.5 if the vertical axis had no values on it? Because of their misleading nature, truncated graphs which are used inappropriately are known as 'gee-whizz graphs'. One of the best sources for them (although by no means the only one) tends to be newspaper advertisements and you might like to look at your daily paper with a more critical eye in the future.

Graphing two or more time-series simultaneously

Another interesting problem occurs where two or more sets of time-series data must be graphed together. This might be of use in situations where, for example, we wish to discover whether the series are related and hence move together in some way. In Chapter 12 we will consider some mathematical methods for determining whether a relationship does exist and, if so, how strong it is. However, it is generally useful to begin by graphing the series.

Two basic approaches are open to us. One alternative is to use a double (or triple or whatever) vertical axis. That is to say two series are both plotted using the vertical axis. The simplest approach is probably to use two vertical axes so that one set of figures is read using the left-hand axis and the other set relates to the right-hand axis. An example of this kind of diagram is shown as Figure 2.6. This reproduces a diagram originally published in a *Lloyds Bank Economic Bulletin*. The figure depicts data relating to tourist expenditure in the UK and the £/$ exchange rate. We would perhaps anticipate that tourist expenditure is likely to be strongly affected by changes in the exchange rate and the diagram seems to confirm this.

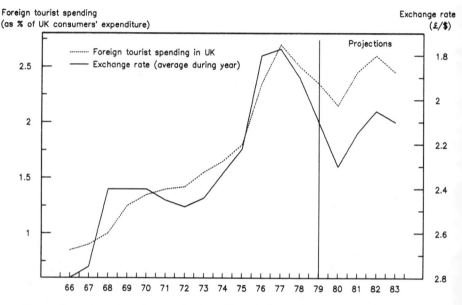

Figure 2.6   *Foreign tourism in the UK and the exchange rate (based on 'Ups and downs of tourism'*, Lloyds Bank Economic Bulletin, *no. 21, September 1980)*

The major advantage of this method of presentation is that it remains possible to read the absolute levels of the variables. However, care must be taken in the interpretation of the graph because the units in which each variable is measured will not be the same. Consider for example the data presented in Table 2.6 relating to the consumption of alcoholic beverages in the UK. Figure 2.7 depicts the data set using a separate vertical axis for each category. Looking at this diagram it is tempting to conclude that wine consumption was greater than that of beer in all years over the period. The error here is that wine consumption is measured using millions of *gallons* whereas beer consumption is in terms of millions of *bulk barrels*. Unless we know therefore how many gallons there are in a bulk barrel, it is impossible to say anything about comparative levels of consumption. What is clear from the graph is that wine and spirit consumption increased much faster than beer consumption.

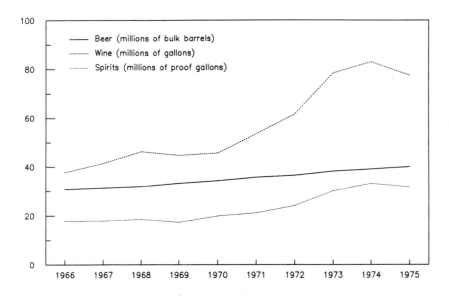

Figure 2.7 *UK alcoholic liquor consumption 1966–75*

Table 2.6 *UK alcoholic liquor consumption 1966–1975*

	1966	*1967*	*1968*	*1969*	*1970*	*1971*	*1972*	*1973*	*1974*	*1975*
Beer										
(millions of bulk barrels)	30.8	31.4	32.0	33.4	34.4	35.8	36.6	38.3	39.1	40.1
Index numbers	76.8	78.3	79.8	83.3	85.8	89.3	91.3	95.5	97.5	100.0
Wine										
(millions of gallons)	37.7	41.6	46.4	44.9	45.8	53.8	61.9	78.4	82.9	77.5
Index numbers	48.7	53.7	59.9	57.9	59.1	69.4	79.9	101.2	107.0	100.0
Spirits										
(millions of proof gallons)	17.8	17.9	18.6	17.5	20.0	21.2	24.4	30.2	33.2	31.7
Index numbers	56.2	56.5	58.7	55.2	3.1	66.9	76.3	95.3	104.7	100.0

Source: Basic data from Medlik, S. and Airey,   (1978), *Profile of the Hotel and Catering Industry* 2nd edn, Butterworth–Heinei ann, p. 115.
Note: Base year for index numbers = 1975.

The second way in which two sets of data may be depicted on the same diagram is to convert all the data to a common vertical scale. The way in which this is done is to present each data set as a series of index numbers. This is quite a straightforward process, but the graph requires even more careful interpretation than the multiple vertical scale. Essentially, with index numbers, rather than plotting the actual values of the data, each point of a series is plotted as a value *relative* to some arbitrarily chosen base value of the same series. One year is chosen as the base year and all values are calculated as percentages of this value. For each year the appropriate index numbers may be calculated by using the following formula:

$$\text{Index no. for year } y = \frac{\text{value for year } y}{\text{value in base year}} \times 100$$

Suppose, for example, that 1975 is taken as the base year. The index numbers are presented in Table 2.6. It may be seen that each series builds towards a value of 100. If we plot the index numbers as in Figure 2.8 it is again tempting to infer something about the absolute levels of consumption (for example that beer consumption was greater than wine or spirits in 1966 but that the consumption of all three was the same in 1975). Once again this kind of conclusion is incorrect. All that the graph shows is the way in which each series built up to its 1975 value – i.e. the increase in beer consumption was much slower than either of the other two. Interestingly the graph also shows that the *percentage* increase in the consumption of wines and spirits over the period was rather similar. This is not obvious from the graph of absolute values (Figure 2.7).

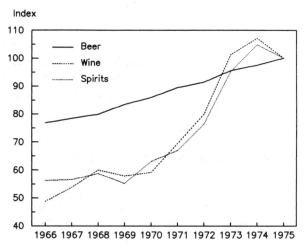

Figure 2.8   *UK alcoholic liquor consumption (index numbers)*

The presentation of rates of change may also be achieved by using 'log paper' i.e. graph paper where either the vertical axis (semi-log) or both axes (log-log) are plotted using a log scale rather than a natural scale. The terminology log scale is sometimes off-putting. It merely means that the axis instead of increasing 1, 2, 3, etc. as usual, increases 10^1, 10^2, 10^3, etc. In other words, it is the powers (or logs) rather than the numbers that determine the scale.

Using the absolute values and plotting them on semi-log paper gives Figure 2.9. Once again the relative changes in consumption are clear.

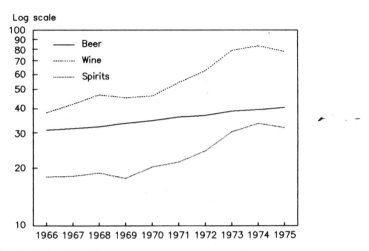

Figure 2.9   *UK alcoholic liquor consumption (log scale)*

Whichever of these methods is adopted, the graph is restricted to highlighting the relationship between changes in the variables. The only time that anything may be inferred about the absolute levels of the variables is when they are measured in the same units, in which case a single vertical axis may be used.

Other methods of data presentation

Before leaving this chapter, some other common data presentation methods, used for instance in company reports, will be reviewed.

First, there is the relatively well-known *pie chart* wherein a circle is used to depict the total data set and this is then divided into parts according to some criterion. In the past drawing pie charts tended to be a relatively tedious process, but nowadays most statistical computer packages include routines for drawing 'exploding' pie charts. The use of pie charts is nonetheless rather limited. They are best used when the number of categories is fairly small. If a large number of categories is present many of them will probably be small and the diagram will simply become confusing. In such circumstances it is probably better to proceed either by combining some categories or by using a histogram instead.

A second common method of data presentation especially favoured by companies in their reports is the pictogram. Here some object is chosen to represent the data – for instance, a fish might be used to represent the number of fish and chip dinners sold. The scope for confusion with pictograms seems to be endless (which may have something to do with their popularity!). The best way of using them is to let the picture represent a standard value of the variable – for example, one fish might represent 10 fish dinners sold. If the hotel sells 100 such meals then this would be shown as 10 fish. The difficulties begin when 97 meals are sold which must be shown as 9 and 7/10 fish. All kinds of strange interpretation may be put upon the fraction of the fish! The worst usage of pictograms is when the chosen object simply increases or decreases in size with the data. For instance, we may draw a fish to represent 10 dinners and one which is 10 times larger to show 100 dinners. Of course we fall into the 'volume trap' as shown by Figure 2.1 – with the added complication that the object itself may confuse matters. People may simply come away with the idea that where once the hotel served sardines it now serves whales! By and large pictograms are probably best avoided.

Conclusion

This chapter has looked at the organization and presentation of data. While it is to be hoped that you will have mastered all the techniques discussed, probably the single most important aspect is the organization of data. You should be able to take a 'raw' data set and classify it in such a way as to produce a clear and accurate summary of the original data. You should also be able to understand and critically assess the way in which data are presented by other people. If you have any doubts about data classification re-read the relevant sections of the chapter before proceeding further in the book. Much of the material to come depends on your understanding the principles of data classification so that resolving now any problems you may have will save you time in the long run.

Of the data presentation methods considered, by far the most important is the histogram. Much of the subject matter of statistics revolves around histograms in various guises, so once again if you have any doubts about the concept resolve your difficulties before proceeding further.

Having considered then how data may be organized and summarized visually, let us now go on to consider the way in which a data set may be summarized using numerical methods.

References and further reading

Only the most important data presentation methods have been covered in this chapter. Some more esoteric methods are included in:

HUFF, D. (1986), *How to Lie with Statistics*, Pelican.
YEOMANS, K. (1968), *Statistics for the Social Scientist*, Penguin, 2 vols.

An interesting article related to one topic covered in this chapter is:

ARBEL, A. and GELLER, A. (1983), 'Foreign exchange sensitivity: how a strong currency weakens hotel revenues', *Cornell HRA Quarterly*, November, pp. 64–70.

Exercises

1   A sample of 100 salaries taken from payroll records gives the following data set:

16,200	8,200	11,000	8,000	11,300
12,000	10,400	12,400	5,600	5,200
11,800	25,300	7,850	14,100	12,000
8,900	11,250	13,200	9,100	13,200
10,500	12,000	15,400	6,500	7,300
4,600	12,350	17,000	11,600	7,800
10,500	7,800	12,500	8,900	9,200
16,250	10,250	17,890	13,550	8,900
24,000	9,000	9,200	16,200	12,400
10,790	10,900	10,500	16,000	6,800
14,500	8,000	8,250	9,200	15,250
10,250	16,000	7,500	13,600	12,730
16,800	14,500	10,000	4,450	10,800
4,800	9,000	28,300	6,500	15,600
12,550	9,000	6,300	10,250	5,200
16,900	8,200	8,500	22,000	8,000
7,700	11,000	4,700	8,248	10,800
23,500	12,400	10,000	6,390	13,250
6,800	6,000	10,250	7,300	14,700
7,790	12,250	7,800	14,950	8,270

(a) Classify the data.
(b) Draw the histogram.
(c) Discuss the advantages and disadvantages of data classification.

2   An industrial catering company is testing one of its can-filling machines. The stated weight on the can is 1 kg. A sample of 120 cans inspected gives the following results in grammes:

1000	1003	1001	1003	1004	1001	1004	998
1002	1005	1006	999	1003	996	1002	1006
1000	1003	1006	1005	998	1006	1009	1003
999	1007	1004	1008	1000	1009	1002	1000
1001	997	1006	1007	1001	1004	1008	1001
1004	1002	1006	1005	1001	1004	1003	1004
1001	1005	1010	1004	1004	1006	1002	1006
999	1003	1006	1000	1004	1007	998	1002
1009	1005	1005	1003	1010	1007	1002	1005
998	1002	1006	1003	1008	1004	1009	1006
997	1011	1007	999	1005	999	1004	1008
1003	1005	1003	1005	1005	1000	1005	1007
1004	1003	1005	1003	1001	997	1006	1001
1007	1003	1005	1000	1008	997	1004	1007
1002	1004	999	1001	1007	1003	1002	1003

(a) Produce the frequency distribution of the data set.
(b) Draw the frequency histogram.
(c) Calculate the 'less than' cumulative frequency and draw its ogive. Estimate the median weight.
(d) Assuming that the machine is working as intended, it is clear that, to deal with the inherent variability, the company has adopted a strategy of stating a low weight relative to the actual weight of most tins. In this way fewer tins will be rejected as underweight at the quality control stage.
  (i) What other strategies might be followed?
  (ii) What factors will determine the most profitable strategy?
3   Complete the series on hotel employment and present the data:
(a) to show the level of employment;
(b) on a log scale;
(c) to show changes in the level of employment.
4   Bring the data for exchange rates and tourist spending up to date and check the accuracy of Lloyd's Bank's projections. What do you think explains any inaccuracies found?

3
The numerical description of data

The previous chapter presented some ways in which data sets might be organized and depicted graphically as an aid to their interpretation. If, however, we wish to analyse the data, the graphical approach is generally inadequate. Numerical methods for summarizing data sets are therefore required.

The apparent variety of methods that may be used is sometimes confusing. What needs to be emphasized, however, is that there are only two fundamental ideas involved – it is merely that a number of interpretations may be put upon them. Neither of the basic ideas is very difficult to grasp.

Suppose that we have a data set which we wish to summarize numerically. The first thing that we need to know is whether the numbers in the set are mainly large or small – for example, are they in the millions or in the tens? For this we need what is called a *measure of location* – that is a number which gives us an idea of where the data set lies. One way to conceptualize what is meant by a measure of location is to imagine a histogram. To be able to draw a histogram we need to know where on the horizontal axis to plot the bars. The measure of location tells us (roughly) where on the horizontal axis the histogram is situated. Note that the measures of location are sometimes called *measures of central tendency* because they indicate where the centre of the data set (histogram) is located, rather than where it begins.

Knowing the location of the data set is clearly useful but it is not sufficient. Suppose that we are asked to sketch the histogram of a data set comprising 50 observations and centred on a value of 33. How might we go about this? The answer, you will discover if you attempt it, is that we cannot even draw a rough sketch because we have no information on how spread out is the histogram. Hence the second number that we require to be able to summarize a data set is a *measure of dispersion* (or spread). The interpretation of a measure of dispersion is slightly less apparent than that of a measure of location but, as we shall see presently, it is not difficult. For each of the measures of spread used, the same basic principle exists – the larger the number, the more spread is the data set.

Once we know where the data set is located and how spread out it is, we should have a pretty good idea what it looks like without needing to draw it. Of course other summary measures may be useful. For example, many business-related data sets are positively skewed and some measure of this may be helpful. Additional summary measures, like this, may occasionally be necessary, but by and large statistical analysis proceeds by reducing data sets to just two numbers.

In the discussion of measures of location and dispersion, it will be helpful to use an example. For the sake of continuity we will apply the various measures to the same data set throughout this chapter. Other applications are given in the exercises, although the generality of the methods will become apparent as we proceed. We will use as our example the salary structure of a hypothetical hotel group. We will suppose that the data have been presented to us as in Table 3.1.

Table 3.1   *Salary structure of hotel group X*

Salary in pounds (x)	Number of people (f)
4,000 to less than 8,000	92
8,000 to less than 9,000	74
9,000 to less than 10,000	67
10,000 to less than 15,000	60
15,000 to less than 20,000	32
20,000 and above	25

Source: hypothetical data

Measures of location

Three main measures are used – the mode, the median and the arithmetic mean. We shall consider each of these in turn.

The mode

In any given data set, the mode is defined as that observation which occurs most frequently. If the data are not grouped then finding the mode presents no real difficulty. For instance, consider the following simple data set:

$$8, 25, 10, 27, 12, 25, 18, 21, 25 \rightarrow \text{Mode} = 25$$

Because there is only one mode this sample is said to be unimodal. Of course, there is no guarantee that there will only be one mode.

Where the data are not grouped, however, the mode may be quite atypical of the set so that most often the mode is used with grouped data. In this case we identify the modal class which, once the classes have been standardized, is the one with the greatest frequency or if looking at the histogram is simply the tallest one. An estimate of the mode may be made from the histogram as shown in Figure 3.1 (which presents the histogram of the data set in Table 3.1). The top right-hand corner of the modal class is joined to the top right-hand corner of the preceding class and the top left-hand corner of the modal class is joined to the top left-hand corner of the next class. The value of the mode is then read from the horizontal axis at the point where these lines cross. This method gives us an estimate of the mode of about £8,800 (shown in Figure 3.1 as point M).

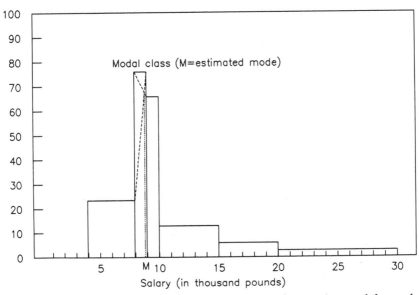

Figure 3.1   *Histogram of salary data (Table 3.1) with an estimate of the mode*

The graphical method of calculating the mode just described may be converted to its formula equivalent fairly readily. In many instances it will prove more convenient to use this formula-based approach than to draw the histogram. It should be noted that we must standardize the class frequencies *as if* we were going to draw the histogram, otherwise the wrong class will be identified as the modal one. For instance, if we use the non-standardized data presented in Table 3.1 then we will identify the first class as being the modal one, since it has the greatest frequency. Once we examine the class widths, it is clear that the correct modal class is the 8,000–

9,000 one. For a standard class width of 1,000 the first class has a standardized frequency of only 23 (as shown in Figure 3.1).

The logic underlying the formula is as follows. Once we have correctly identified the modal class, we know that the mode must lie within its limits. The question is whether it is closer to the lower or upper limit. To answer this question we consider the classes preceding (P) and following (F) the modal one. If P is higher (has a greater frequency) than F then it seems logical to argue that the mode must be closer to the lower limit than the upper limit of the modal class, and the greater is the difference between P and F, the closer must the mode be to the lower limit. If, on the other hand, F is greater than P then the mode will be closer to the upper limit. The derivation of the following formula is based on this reasoning.

Let us denote the lower class boundary of the (standardized) modal class as LCB, the difference between the frequency of the modal class and the class before it as DIF1, the difference between the frequency of the modal class and the class following it as DIF2, and the width of the modal class as WMC. The mode is then given as follows:

$$\text{MODE} = \text{LCB} + \left(\frac{\text{DIF1}}{\text{DIF1} + \text{DIF2}} \times \text{WMC} \right) \tag{3.1}$$

Applying the formula to the salary data shown in Table 3.1 we obtain:

$$\text{MODE} = 8,000 + \left(\frac{51}{58} \times 1,000 \right) = £8,879.31$$

This then is our first measure of the location of the data set, £8,879.31 being the salary that is earned by the greatest number of people.

The method of calculating the mode presented as Equation (3.1) is that which seems to command widest support amongst statisticians. However, other methods do exist. One common approach is merely to take the mid-point of the modal class as the estimate of the mode. This procedure seems less satisfactory than that described here, however, although it will give the correct result if the distribution is symmetrical (or approximately so).

The median

The median represents a second way of approaching the problem of locating a data set. It is defined as the value of the variable (salary in our example) that divides the data set in two – each half having the same *frequency.* Consider the following simple sample:

$$4, 4, 5, 6, 7, 8, 9, 9, 40$$

The median here has a value of 7. There are two important things to notice. First, the sample is written in order. This must always be done or the median will not be identified. Second, the median does *not* equal 22. The error is often made of calculating the 'median' by adding 40 and 4 and then dividing by 2. As is clear from the example above this does not split the data set into two equal parts.

Where the sample has an even number of observations we take the mid-point of the two middle values. For instance, if we take the above sample and ignore the value of 40 then we have only 8 observations. The median would therefore be 6.5 (the mid-point of 6 and 7)

When we are dealing with grouped data (as in Table 3.1), the idea underlying the median remains the same but clearly we can no longer arrange the individual values in order. What we do therefore is to find the value of the variable that has 50% of the frequency either side of it (i.e. the salary that has 50% of people earning less and 50% of people more). To be able to do this we need first to calculate the 'less-than' cumulative (c.f.) and relative cumulative (r.c.f.) frequencies. These are shown in Table 3.2 for our example of the hotel salaries.

Table 3.2   *Cumulative frequency of salary structure of hotel group X*

Salary in pounds (x)	No. of people (f)	Less–than cum. freq.	Relative less- than c.f. (%)
4,000 to less than 8,000	92	92	26.3
8,000 to less than 9,000	74	166	47.4
9,000 to less than 10,000	67	233	66.6
10,000 to less than 15,000	60	293	83.7
15,000 to less than 20,000	32	325	92.9
20,000 and above	25	350	100.0

Source: Table 3.1

As was the case with the mode, we can develop a formula for calculating the median of grouped data. In our sample we have 350 observations so that the median must correspond to the 175th of these. The median class is thus the one that contains the 175th observation. (Alternatively and equivalently it is the one that corresponds to the 50% point of the relative cumulative frequency distribution.) From Table 3.2 we can see that the 175th observation must lie in the 9,000 to less than 10,000 class.

The question is: how far inside the class does it lie? The cumulative frequency shows that the 166th observation lies on the border of the 8,000–9,000 and 9,000–10,000 classes. The median observation is only 9 away from this one (175–166). In the absence of any other information, we assume that the observations inside the median class are evenly spread out. As there are 67 of them, the median observation itself must lie 9/67 of the way into the class. How far is this? It depends on the width of the class. In this case the median class is £1,000 wide and therefore 9/67 of the way into the class corresponds to a value of £134.39. Adding this to the lower class boundary of the median class (£9,000) gives an estimate of the median of £9,134.39.

The logic of the above may be generalized into a formula for the calculation of the median. We shall use the following notation:

LCB   = lower class boundary of the median class
cf(LCB)   = cumulative frequency up to the lower class boundary of the median class (i.e. it tells us the observation that corresponds to the lower class boundary of the median class)
$n/2$ = the median observation
f(med)   = frequency of the median class
w(med)   = width of the median class.

Using this notation we obtain:

$$\text{Median} = \text{LCB} + \left(\frac{n/2 - \text{cf(LCB)}}{f(\text{med})} \times w(\text{med}) \right) \qquad (3.2)$$

And using this formula to calculate the median of our example, gives:

$$\text{Median} = 9,000 + \left(\frac{175 - 166}{67} \times 1,000 \right) = £9,134.39$$

We now have two measures of location for our data set. Let us go on to consider a third possibility.

The arithmetic mean

This measure of location is the one that is commonly known as the 'average' (although in fact this term may be misleading since all the measures of location discussed in this chapter are sometimes referred to as 'averages'). For ungrouped data the arithmetic mean is found by summing the values of the observations and then dividing by the number of observations. Where the data are grouped we use the class marks to represent each observation in a class and then multiply these by the class frequency. The arithmetic mean ($\bar{x}$) is found by summing these values for each class and dividing by the total frequency. This gives the standard formula for the arithmetic mean:

$$\bar{x} = \frac{\Sigma \ (xf)}{\Sigma \ f} = \frac{\Sigma \ (xf)}{n} \tag{3.3}$$

Formula (3.3) is applied to the salary data in Table 3.3.

Table 3.3   *Calculation of arithmetic mean salary of hotel group X*

Salary in pounds	Class marks (x)	No. of people (f)	xf
4,000 to less than 8,000	6,000	92	552,000
8,000 to less than 9,000	8,500	74	629,000
9,000 to less than 10,000	9,500	67	636,500
10,000 to less than 15,000	12,500	60	750,000
15,000 to less than 20,000	17,500	32	560,000
20,000 to less than 30,000	25,000	25	625,000
		$\Sigma f = n = 350$	$\Sigma xf = 3{,}752{,}500$

Source: Table 3.1

$$\text{Mean} = \bar{x} = \frac{3{,}752{,}400}{350} = £10{,}721.43 \qquad \text{(to the nearest penny)}.$$

Hence given the present structure of the hotel group we can say that the arithmetic mean salary is approximately £10,721.43. Notice that this is only approximately so. The reason for the approximation lies in the fact that the class mark is being taken to represent all salaries in a particular class. This assumption is the best that we can make in the absence of any other information but that does not necessarily make it correct. It amounts to assuming that the salaries are evenly distributed within each class. Generally this problem is not serious. However, it will be noted that the final open-ended class has been arbitrarily closed at a value of £30,000. A decision has to be made in such cases otherwise the class mark

cannot be identified and the mean cannot be calculated. As was discussed in the previous chapter there is no right or wrong answer but
clearly the decision will affect the estimate of the mean. As we are dealing
with salaries, perhaps we should make allowance for potentially very

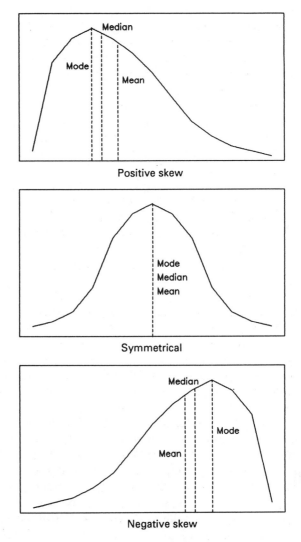

Figure 3.2   *The relationship between measures of location with
different distributions*

high values and close the class at, say, £50,000. The estimate of the mean would now become £11,435.71. We can see then that relatively large changes in the arithmetic mean can occur simply because of changes in our assumptions about open-ended classes.

The relationship between the measures of location

We have looked at three different measures of location. Figure 3.2 summarizes the relationship between them. Where the data set being studied is distributed symmetrically then the three measures will give exactly the same result and it clearly will not matter which one is used. Where, however, the distribution is skewed (either positively or negatively) the three measures no longer give the same answer. The arithmetic mean is pulled towards extreme values (particularly high ones when the distribution is positively skewed). The mode on the other hand is pulled towards the bulk of the observations. In cases where we have skewed distributions, it might be argued that the median provides a better measure of location than either of the other two.

Let us consider further our example above of the hotel group's salary structure. Salaries, like many business-related variables, are typically distributed with a positive skew and this is shown by the data set above. The mode is found to be £8,879.31; the median is £9,134.39 and the mean is £10,721.43 (or £11,435.71 depending on our assumptions concerning the final class). These results accord with the general expectation as shown in Figure 3.2.

We have then three quite different estimates of where the data set is located. Each is perfectly valid and the use to which they are put depends on what one is attempting to do. Suppose for instance that the hotel group is in the middle of a dispute with a trade union regarding salary levels. You are asked by the management to present the case as favourably as possible. You say therefore that the average (mean) salary in the group is £10,721.43 (or even £11,435.71). How can the union possibly claim that salaries are too low? On the other hand, if you are asked by the union to present their case then of course you use the mode and say that most people earn only £8,879.31. How can the group be so mean as to deny the claim for more money? Many trade disputes seem to proceed in this kind of semantic manner, even if the two sides are generally more subtle than this.

In statistics, the arithmetic mean is the most important of the measures of location. There are a number of reasons for this. First, much of statistics concerns inferences made about populations on the basis of samples drawn from them. An important theorem of statistics shows that if a sample is large enough it will have an approximately symmetrical (normal) distribution regardless of the distribution of the population from which it is taken.

In this case, the arithmetic mean is sufficient as a measure of location. Second, the arithmetic mean is a more consistent measure of location than the other two – that is to say, if repeated samples are taken from a population and the three measures of location are calculated for each sample, the arithmetic mean will be less variable than the other two. Third, the mean makes use of all the information contained in the sample. Fourth, the mean has proven much easier to develop mathematically than the other two measures. For these reasons, the arithmetic mean has dominated in the development of statistics and it is the measure of location that will generally be used in the remainder of this book.

Measures of dispersion

Having discussed some of the measures of location, we now turn our attention to the second important numerical descriptor required to summarize a data set – the measure of dispersion. The purpose of this is to indicate how spread out is the data set. We know where it is located and we need then to know the spread around this location. A number of possible measures are available.

The range

One way of describing dispersion might be to give the range – that is the difference between the largest and smallest values in the data set. The clear difficulty with this approach is that we only use two observations from the set available to us and these two may not be especially representative. For instance, the two distributions below have the same range and yet clearly differ substantially.

0, 50, 100 Range = 100
0, 48, 48, 48, 50, 50, 52, 52, 52, 100 Range = 100

Intuitively it is obvious that the first data set is much more variable than the second, yet our measure of dispersion (the range) tells us that the degree of dispersion is the same in both cases. Clearly a measure such as this will not suffice.

Sometimes, in an attempt to rescue the idea of the range, the interquartile range is used instead. Recall that the median corresponds to the value of the variable that has 50% of observations either side of it. The interquartile range uses the 25% and 75% values and then differences these. Of course this procedure, although it may often give a better result, does not cure the basic fault with the range that only two values are considered.

The mean absolute deviation from the mean

If we are interested in finding out how spread out is a particular data set then one approach is to begin by calculating a measure of location, and then to consider each observation in the data set in turn and see how far they are from this point. This method is usually applied using the arithmetic mean as the measure of location, although in principle any such measure could be used.

Consider the two example data sets presented in the previous section. The arithmetic mean ($\bar{x}$) is 50 in both cases. If we calculate the difference between each successive observation (x) and the mean ($\bar{x}$) for each data set, we obtain the results shown in Table 3.4.

Table 3.4   *The difference between observations and mean value*

Example data set 1		Example data set 2	
x	$x-\bar{x}$	x	$x-\bar{x}$
0	−50	0	−50
50	0	48	− 2
100	50	48	− 2
		48	− 2
		50	0
		50	0
		52	2
		52	2
		52	2
		100	50

We have now calculated the set of deviations from the mean. This does not get us very far, however. What we require is a single measure to describe the degree of dispersion of the entire data set. An obvious procedure is to sum the deviations. However, in both of the above cases this sum is zero because the distributions are symmetrical around the mean, so that the positive and negative deviations counterbalance one another. To overcome this problem we consider the absolute deviations only (i.e. we ignore the signs) and we sum these. This gives the total absolute deviation from the mean (TAD). It may be tempting to argue that we could use this value as our measure of dispersion – the implication being that the higher the total absolute deviation, the more spread the data set. The flaw in this argument is that as we add more observations to the data set the total deviation almost always increases even if intuitively the degree of spread is falling. In our examples above, the TAD of the first data set is 100 and that of the second 112. This difference is due simply to the fact that the second data set has more observations than the first.

To overcome the above problem we calculate the arithmetic mean of the absolute deviations – that is, we divide the TAD by the number of observations. We end up with the *mean absolute deviation from the mean* (MAD). In the case of the data sets presented in Table 3.4, the MAD of the first set is 33.3 (100/3) while that of the second set is 11.2 (112/10). We now have a summary measure of dispersion which accords with the common-sense view that the first data set is more spread than the second.

The discussion so far may be summarized in the following formula:

$$\text{MAD} = \frac{|x - \bar{x}|}{n} \tag{3.4}$$

Where the MAD is used with grouped data, the x's become the class marks and the difference between each class mark and the mean must be multiplied by the frequency (f) of the class giving:

$$\text{MAD} = \frac{[|x - \bar{x}| \times f]}{n} \tag{3.5}$$

In Table 3.5, this formula is applied to the salary data. We obtain:

Table 3.5   *Calculation of mean absolute deviation from the mean*

| | Salaries in hotel group X | | |
Class marks (x)	x − x̄	No. of people (f)	|x − x̄| × f
6,000	−4,721.43	92	434,371.56
8,500	−2,221.43	74	164,385.82
9,500	−1,221.43	67	81,835.81
12,500	1,778,57	60	106,714.20
17,500	6,778.57	32	216,914.24
25,000	14,278.57	25	356,964.25
		$\Sigma = 350$	$\Sigma = 1,361,185.88$

Source: Table 3.1

$$\text{MAD} = \frac{1,361,185.88}{350} = £3,889.10$$

The advantage of the MAD is that we now have a measure that makes use of all the information that we have available. The interpretation of the MAD is straightforward, although at first sight not particularly revealing: on the average, each observation is £3,889.10 away from the mean value.

A more useful interpretation is to say that in a symmetrical distribution, approximately 50% of the observations will be within a range of one MAD either side of the mean. This gives a better idea of the spread of the values.

The MAD suffers, however, from a drawback that has rather limited its usage. Because we are dealing with absolute values it is very difficult to develop the formula mathematically. For instance, each time that we add a new observation to the data set we must recalculate the mean and then recalculate all deviations from it. When a large data set is involved the process may become very time consuming even where a computer is available.

The variance and the standard deviation

The variance and standard deviation are concepts that are related to the MAD and which also build upon the idea of the deviation from the mean. It will be recalled that the basic problem with the deviation from the mean was that the deviations intially summed to zero (for a symmetrical distribution). The MAD tackled this problem by considering only the absolute values. An alternative method of removing the signs is to square all values and this is the approach adopted by the variance and the standard deviation.

We begin then by squaring all deviations from the mean. We then sum them and divide by the number of observations. This procedure should give, in keeping with our previous terminology, the 'mean squared deviation from the mean'. Somewhat confusingly however this concept is called the *variance*. Finally, we have the problem that because we have squared everything our units are now also squared. To return to our original units we must therefore square root the variance. This quantity is called the *standard deviation*, which is perhaps easier than the 'square root of the mean squared deviation from the mean'.

The above logic may easily be translated into a formula for the calculation of the two values. The formula presented is for the case where we have grouped data – with ungrouped data, the fs are merely removed (or more accurately set equal to one). Generally speaking, the variance and standard deviation will be calculated with respect to a sample rather than to a complete statistical population. In this case, we divide by $n - 1$ rather than n since otherwise the sample variance tends to underestimate the true population variance.

$$\text{Variance} = \quad s^2 = \frac{\Sigma \, [\, (\, x - \bar{x} \,)^2 \times f \,]}{n - 1} \qquad (3.6)$$

$$\text{Standard deviation} = \quad s = \sqrt{s^2} \tag{3.7}$$

The procedure used to calculate the standard deviation is to calculate first the variance and then to square root the answer. Notice that so far the standard deviation suffers the same drawback as the MAD in that we need to know the mean to be able to calculate it. If therefore we add an observation to our sample, the mean is likely to change and everything will have to be recalculated from scratch. For this reason the above formulae should be thought of as definitions – except with very small data sets they should not be used for calculations. The great advantage of the variance and standard deviation is that it is possible to develop the above formulae so as to eliminate the mean. (See the appendix to this chapter for a proof of this.) We then obtain the following formula for the variance:

$$s^2 = \frac{\Sigma (x^2 f) - ((\Sigma xf)^2/n)}{n - 1} \tag{3.8}$$

Now if further observations are added, the various totals are simply increased without the need to recalculate the whole problem. A significant amount of time is thereby saved. Applying Formula (3.8) to the salary data, we obtain Table 3.6.

Table 3.6   *Calculation of variance and standard deviation*

		Salaries in hotel group X		
Class marks (x)	x^2	No. of people (f)	xf	x^2f
6,000	36,000,000	92	552,000	3,312,000,000
8,500	72,250,000	74	629,000	5,346,500,000
9,500	90,250,000	67	636,500	6,046,750,000
12,500	156,250,000	60	750,000	9,375,000,000
17,500	306,250,000	32	560,000	9,800,000,000
25,000	625,000,000	25	625,000	15,625,000,000
		350	3,752,500	49,505,250,000

Source: Table 3.1

$$s^2 \quad = \quad \frac{[\, 49,505,250,000 - (3,752,500^2 / 350)\,]}{349}$$

$$= \frac{[\ 49,505,250,000\ -\ (14,081,256,250,000\ /\ 350)\ ]}{349}$$

$$= 26,570,456$$

The standard deviation of the salary data is thus found by square rooting the variance to be £5,154.65. The calculations have been shown in some detail above to demonstrate how cumbersome they may become even when using the computational formula on a relatively small data set. For this reason, means and standard deviations are often calculated using a computer. Where a computer is not available, the calculations can be greatly simplified using the method of the assumed mean (also known as linear transformation or coding). Before turning to these aids in computation, we will briefly discuss the relationship between the mean and the standard deviation. This will help clarify the meaning of the standard deviation, which as might be expected is similar to the MAD.

The relationship between the mean and standard deviation

Many phenomena have distributions that are symmetrical about their mean. That is to say, if we plot out the data set we obtain a diagram such as Figure 3.3. In this case the standard deviation has a particular interpretation.

We note that the distribution is centred on (located at) the arithmetic mean. The standard deviation then tells us how the distribution is spread around the mean. If we add one standard deviation to the mean and subtract one then about 67% of the observations in the data set should lie within this range. Within the range of the mean plus and minus two standard deviations we should have about 95% of observations. And finally between 3 standard deviations either side we should have about 99% of observations.

For a given value of the mean, a low value of the standard deviation indicates a tightly distributed data set (i.e. observations are at or near the mean) whereas a high value of the standard deviation indicates a spread out data set. Note however that the terms 'high' and 'low' when applied to a standard deviation have to be applied in a relative sense. In particular we must consider the standard deviation in relation to the mean. Suppose that we have two data sets each with a standard deviation of 25. This does not necessarily mean that they are equally spread out. Suppose that the first data set has a mean of 25 whereas the second has a mean of 2,500,000. It is intuitively clear that the first data set is relatively more variable than the second. It seems a fairly obvious step then to describe the relative variability of data sets by taking the standard deviation as a proportion of the mean, and this is what statisticians have done.

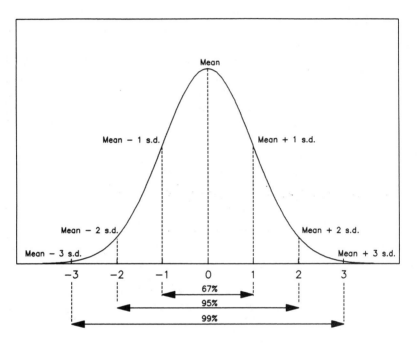

Figure 3.3   *The relationship between mean and standard deviation*

The coefficient of variation

One measure of relative variability is the coefficient of variation which is given as:

$$v = s \,/\, \bar{x} \qquad\qquad (3.9)$$

Generally the answer is multiplied by 100 so that v is expressed as a percentage. Considering the two simple examples given earlier we have

$$v = 25/25 = 1 \times 100 = 100\% \qquad \text{and,}$$

$$v = 25/2500000 = 0.00001 \times 100 = 0.001\%$$

As we have already observed the first data set is substantially more variable than the second. Note therefore that where we wish to compare two or more data sets we must use the coefficient of variation rather than ✓ just the standard deviation if we are interested in relative variability.

Linear transformation

As was demonstrated in Table 3.6, the calculations necessary for the computation of the mean and, especially, the standard deviation may become very unwieldly. In many cases, they cannot be performed accurately using a standard calculator. One solution is to use a computer (see the following section). However, in many situations the calculations may be greatly simplified by using the method of linear transformation. The basic idea is straightforward. Essentially our difficulties arise because the numbers are too large. Another way of looking at this problem is to argue that the distribution is located in the wrong place, i.e. it is too far along the horizontal axis. Why not therefore move the whole distribution back to where the numbers are small, perform the calculations and then transfer the answer back to its correct location? This is essentially what coding involves.

Strictly speaking, the method involves defining a new variable, usually called u, which is related to our original variable x, by the equation:

$$u = \frac{x - a}{b}$$

The mean and the standard deviation are then calculated for the u variable. The results are then translated back to our original units using the relationships:

$$\bar{x} = a + b\bar{u}$$

$$s_x = |b| \, s_u$$

where $|b|$ is the absolute value of b.

The values a and b are arbitrary. The secret of success is to choose those values that make the calculations as simple as possible. Generally, it is helpful to make a equal to one of the x values so that the corresponding u

value becomes zero and this row then disappears from the calculation. It is also often a good idea to pick a middle x value so that the positive and negative u values balance out. There are no such ground rules in the case of b which can be any number, positive or negative, whole or fraction.

To demonstrate the use of coding we will apply it in Table 3.7 to the data concerning the hotel group salaries. The value of a is set to 9,500 and b to 1,000.

Table 3.7   *Calculation of mean and standard deviation using linear transformation*

		Salaries in hotel group X			
		$u = \dfrac{x - a}{b}$			
Class marks (x)	No. of people (f)		u^2	uf	u^2f
6,000	92	− 3.5	12.25	− 322	1127
8,500	74	− 1	1	− 74	74
9,500	67	0	0	0	0
12,500	60	3	9	180	540
17,500	32	8	64	256	2048
25,000	25	15.5	240.25	387.5	6006.25
	350			427.5	9795.25

Source: Table 3.1

$$\bar{u} = \frac{427.5}{350} = 1.2214286$$

$$\bar{x} = a + b\bar{u} = 9{,}500 + 1{,}000 \times 1.2214286 = £10{,}721.43 \qquad \text{(as before)}$$

$$s^2u = \frac{[\,9795.25 - (427.5^2 / 350)\,]}{349} = \frac{9273.0893}{349} = 26.570456$$

$$s_u = \sqrt{s^2_u} = \sqrt{26.570456} = 5.1546539$$

$$s_x = |\,b\,|\,s_u = 1{,}000 \times 5.1546539 = £5{,}154.65 \qquad \text{(as before)}$$

It can be seen then that precisely the same answers as before are obtained but the degree of computation is significantly reduced.

The use of computer packages

A number of computer packages are available for the calculation of means and standard deviations. The calculations presented in Table 3.6 were performed using the Lotus Symphony spreadsheet. This allows accurate calculations to be made.

The following output was produced via the SPSS package. The data were first entered via Symphony and were then translated to SPSS format. The descriptives command was then used to obtain the mean and standard deviation. In what follows, the commands issued to SPSS are printed in bold typeface and the output produced by SPSS is printed normally.

translate from = 'c: symph data hot3.wrl'
/fieldnames.
list.

SALARY FREQUENC

6000.0	92.0
8500.0	74.0
9500.0	67.0
12500.0	60.0
17500.0	32.0
25000.0	25.0

Number of cases read =   6   Number of cases listed =   6

weight by frequenc.
descriptive salary.
Number of Valid Observations (Listwise) =   350.00

Variable	Mean	Std Dev	Minimum	Maximum	N
SALARY	10721.43	5154.65	6000.0	25000.0	350

If you have access to SPSS or another statistics package you will find that the above calculations are completed by the computer in a few seconds. While this makes use of the computer extremely attractive, it is essential that you check that the answer makes sense. Not infrequently, the computer serves simply to calculate (very quickly) mistakes. This is especially so where a complex package such as SPSS is used. It is easy to forget a command so that the computer calculates something rather different to what you had intended. For example, if the weight command is omitted, we get:

descriptives salary.

Number of Valid Observations (Listwise) =   6.00

Variable	Mean	Std Dev	Minimum	Maximum	N
SALARY	13166.67	7011.89	6000.0	25000.0	6

Although this is incorrect, the values given for the mean and standard deviation are not absurd and it would be easy to accept them as being correct. The omission of the weights command has led the computer to calculate the mean and standard deviation of the class marks rather than the data set. This is shown by the number of valid observations as 6 (that is the number of classes) rather than the 350 that we should have. Great care is therefore required that the correct problem is being solved by the computer.

Conclusion

Having seen in this and the previous chapter how data sets may be organized and presented pictorially and numerically, we will move on to consider how statistical methods may be used to help business decision making. It must be emphasized once again that the material covered so far is vitally important for correct application of the analytical methods which follow. Almost always statistical work begins with a sample data set which must be organized and summarized before analysis can commence. The methods used for this organization and summary are those that have been covered in these two chapters. If a data set is poorly or incorrectly summarized, it is clear that the analysis based on it is not going to be very fruitful.

The link between the sample data set and the topic being studied is provided by probability and it is to that topic that we now turn.

Exercises

1   Using your classification of the data sets presented in Exercises 1 and 2 following Chapter 2, calculate:

(a) the mode;
(b) the median;
(c) the arithmetic mean.

Using these values, sketch the frequency curve for the two data sets.

2 A trade union has collected the following data regarding salaries earned by those who are members of a union compared with those who are not.

Salary	Union members	Non-union members
Under 10,000	65	85
10,000 to <12,000	45	65
12,000 to <15,000	40	30
15,000 to <20,000	14	8
20,000 and over	12	8

(a) Draw a graph (e.g. a histogram) showing the two data sets.
(b) Calculate the arithmetic mean salary of the two groups.
(c) Calculate the variance and standard deviation of the two groups.
(d) What interpretations might be put upon the results?

Appendix
The derivation of the computational equation for the variance

By definition $\quad s^2 = \dfrac{\Sigma\,(x - \bar{x})^2 f}{n - 1}$ (1)

Hence $\quad s^2 = \dfrac{(x_1 - \bar{x})^2 f_1 + (x_2 - \bar{x})^2 f_2 + \,.....\, + (x_n - \bar{x})^2 fn}{n - 1}$ (2)

Expanding $\quad s^2 = \dfrac{(x^2_1 f_1 - 2\bar{x}x_1 f_1 + \bar{x}^2 f_1) + \,....\, + (x^2_n f_n - 2\bar{x}x_n f_n + \bar{x}^2 f_n)}{n - 1}$ (3)

Simplifying $\quad s^2 = \dfrac{(\Sigma x^2 f - 2\bar{x}\Sigma xf + \Sigma f\bar{x}^2)}{n - 1}$ (4)

But $\bar{x} = \Sigma xf \,/\, n$ and $\Sigma f = n$

Substituting $\quad s^2 = \dfrac{(\Sigma x^2 f - 2\Sigma xf/n\,\,\Sigma xf + n(\Sigma xf/n)^2)}{n - 1}$ (5)

Simplifying $\quad s^2 = \dfrac{(\Sigma x^2 f - 2(\Sigma xf)^2/n + (\Sigma xf)^2/n)}{n - 1}$ (6)

Hence $\quad s^2 = \dfrac{\Sigma x^2 f - (\Sigma xf)^2/n}{n - 1}$ (7)

Equation 7 is the computational equation presented in the chapter. As can be seen, it is derived directly from an expansion of the definition of the variance. As was shown in the main text of the chapter, this derivation greatly facilitates calculation of the variance and standard deviation.

4
An introduction to probability

The previous two chapters have shown how we might organize a data set and summarize it both pictorially and numerically. These aspects of statistics are very important and insufficient emphasis is often put upon them. However, having mastered the descriptive aspects of statistics, we may now pass on to what is generally considered the most interesting and useful part of the subject – analytical, or inferential, statistics.

This part of statistics is concerned with making predictions about a particular population on the basis of a sample drawn from that population. In the next chapter we will consider how this sample should be constructed. Before this it is helpful to consider the basic ideas of probability. In most business situations it is simply too expensive to contact everyone who is affected by a decision (even if we could identify them) so that decisions must be made on the basis of incomplete information. Once information is not complete we find ourselves in uncertain or risky situations. It is here that statistics may be most helpful in business decision making. The link between the sample and the population is provided by probability.

The fundamental principle of probability

The basic principle underlying probability is best explained via a trivial example. (It might be noted at this point that many of the examples used in statistics involve card games or dice. This is not because statisticians are necessarily inveterate gamblers – although of course most of them are! – but rather because the odds may be calculated precisely in these games. It is also true that the study of various games of 'chance' gave much of the initial impetus to the development of probability theory.)

Suppose that we wish to find the probability of obtaining one head if we flip an unbiased coin twice. One way of proceeding is to write out all possible outcomes and then to note which of these gives us our desired result (i.e. which are favourable). In this example we have the following:

total possible outcomes : HH HT TH TT

Of the four possible outcomes, two (HT, TH) give us the required result (one head). We may either get the head with the first throw or the second. It is important to notice that we distinguish between the two outcomes TH and HT. Some students argue that there is only one outcome here – one head and one tail. In a sense this is true, it is just that this outcome may appear in two ways. Another way of looking at the problem is to notice that we did not specify the order when we said one head. If we had specified head on the first throw and tails on the second then there would indeed be only one favourable outcome – HT.

In the original problem we have then two favourable from four possible outcomes. Probability is defined as the ratio of the former to the latter.

$$\text{Probability (one head)} = \frac{\text{favourable outcomes}}{\text{possible outcomes}} = \frac{2}{4} = \frac{1}{2}$$

In more general notation, if we consider some experiment which has n possible outcomes of which m are favourable to an event A then the probability (P) of A occurring is given as:

$$P(A) = m/n$$

This equation summarizes the topic of probability that often seems so tricky. In some instances it may be very difficult, time-consuming, expensive, tedious or simply impossible to calculate exactly the total possible outcomes of an experiment or even those that are favourable. To aid with the counting of outcomes a number of methods have been developed. These methods will be discussed in subsequent chapters of the book. It is important, however, not to lose sight of the fact that the reason why such methods are used is to arrive at an answer to the fraction above.

The probability fraction has some interesting characteristics. First, it can never be less than zero. The worst that can happen is that there are no favourable outcomes in which case the probability equals zero. Second, it can never exceed one, since the best that can happen is that every possible outcome is favourable. For most events, therefore, the probability will have a value between nought and one. This result also acts as a useful control. If you find a probability of, for example, 2.12 then you can be certain (Prob = 1) that it is wrong! Third, if all possible outcomes to an experiment are taken into account then the sum of their probabilities must equal one, since one of them is certain to occur. This result is very useful. If it proves difficult or laborious to calculate the probability that an event, A, occurs, then it often helps to find the probability that A does *not* occur. This is called the complementary event and is denoted as $\overline{A}$. ✓ Since either A or $\overline{A}$ is certain to occur then we have:

$$P(A) + P(\overline{A}) = 1$$

from which it follows immediately that:

$$P(\overline{A}) = 1 - P(A) \quad \text{and} \quad P(\overline{A}) = 1 - P(A)$$

This result is frequently applied in the solution to probability problems.

The addition theorem of probability

Quite often it is useful to break a problem into a number of parts before attempting to solve it. We then calculate the probabilities of the component parts and put these together to obtain the final result. Depending on the nature of the problem under consideration, one of two fundamental theorems of probability may be used. We will consider the addition theorem in this section and the multiplication theorem in the next.

Consider two events – A and B. Suppose that we wish to calculate the probability of *either* one *or* the other occurring. The problem is most easily understood by referring to the Venn diagram (Figure 4.1). If either A or B will do then it is clear from the diagram that we must add the probabilities together (i.e. we require P(A∪B) – the probability of A union B). However, just adding them together will overstate the case because there is some chance that the two events will occur at the same time (i.e. A intersection B). Hence what we must do is calculate the probabilities of A and B occurring separately and then subtract the probability that they occur simultaneously. This gives us the addition theorem of probability:

$$P(A∪B) = P(A) + P(B) - P(A∩B)$$

Consider a simple example. Suppose that a hotel has 200 guests registered. Of these 200, 50 are French and 150 are English. Half of the French guests and half of the English guests are women. If someone gets stuck in the lift what is the probability that the person is EITHER French OR a woman. To calculate this probability we *may* use the addition theorem, although note once again that we do not *have* to do so – it is simply a method of calculating the probability fraction. We can always proceed from fundamental principles.

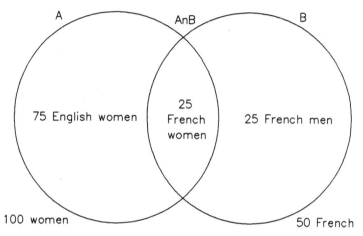

Figure 4.1   *Venn diagram showing union and intersection of two sets*

Let us define event A as being that the person is a woman and event B that the person is French. We shall begin by calculating the probability of events A and B, which are:

$$P(A) = 100/200 \qquad P(B) = 50/200$$

If we were simply to add these two probabilities, we would get 150/200 as our answer. However, this would overstate the true probability. We must remember to subtract the intersection, which in this case is French-women. If we do not subtract this group then they will be double-counted – once as women and once as French. Since half of the French guests are women we have:

$$P(A∩B) = 25/200$$

Hence

$$P(A∪B) = 100/200 + 50/200 - 25/200 = 125/200$$

It is apparent from the calculations above that the Venn diagram represents one method of counting the favourable outcomes in a problem. If you find it helpful then use it. Since there are 125 favourable outcomes, logically there must be 75 unfavourable ones. As a check on your solution, it is often useful to verify that the implied number of unfavourable outcomes is correct. In this case the 75 represent people who are neither French nor women – that is to say, English men – and there are indeed 75 of these. Hence we may be confident that our solution is correct.

If events *A* and *B* are *mutually exclusive* – i.e. they cannot occur together – then the addition theorem is simplified since $P(A \cap B) = 0$. For instance, continuing the previous example suppose we wish to find the probability that the person is either a French man or an English woman. Clearly the two events are mutually exclusive. It is not possible to be a French man and an English woman at the same time (even if it may be possible with the miracles of modern diplomacy and modern medicine to be them consecutively). Hence in this case:

$$P(A \cup B) = P(A) + P(B) = 25/100 + 75/100 = 100/200$$

The multiplication theorem of probability

The addition theorem is concerned with situations where *either* of the events will suffice. The multiplication theorem looks at problems where *both* events must occur. The basic idea can best be demonstrated via an example. Suppose that a local company is to hold a banquet and has asked three hotels (*A*, *B* and *C*) to tender for it. If both hotel *A* and hotel *B* belong to the same chain, what is the probability that the chain wins the bid? This is an application of the addition theorem that we have just looked at since the chain wins if *either* hotel A *or* hotel B is awarded the contract. Assuming that each hotel is equally likely to win (i.e. $P(A) = P(B) = P(C) = 1/3$) then the chain has a 2/3 chance of winning.

Now suppose that two companies are asking for quotes for banquets from hotels *A*, *B* and *C*. What is the probability that the same hotel will win both bids? This is an application of the multiplication theorem. To calculate the overall probability, we multiply together the probabilities of the component parts (i.e. probability of winning bid 1 multiplied by probability of winning bid 2). Again supposing each hotel to be equally likely to win each bid then we have:

$$P(\text{both bids}) = P(\text{bid 1}) \times P(\text{bid 2}) = 1/3 \times 1/3 = 1/9$$

Hence each of the hotels has a 1 in 9 chance of winning both contracts. We can demonstrate that this is correct using a tree diagram (Figure 4.2). This is a graphical method of identifying possible and favourable outcomes to a problem. Consider first bid 1. There are 3 possible outcomes *A, B* or *C*. If the hotel chain owns 2 of the three hotels, then it has 2 favourable outcomes and thus the probability of its winning the bid is 2/3.

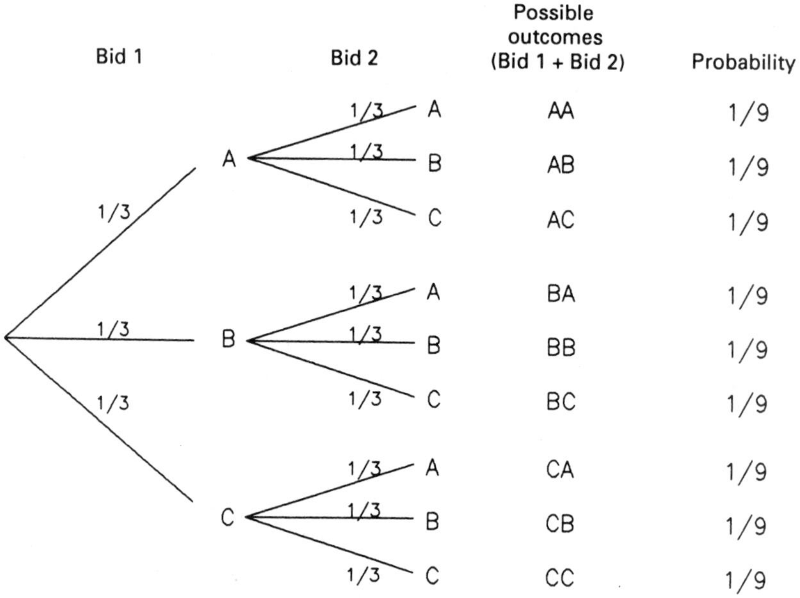

Bid 1	Bid 2	Possible outcomes (Bid 1 + Bid 2)	Probability
	1/3 — A	AA	1/9
A 1/3 — B	AB	1/9
1/3	1/3 ⟍ C	AC	1/9
	1/3 — A	BA	1/9
1/3 — B 1/3 — B	BB	1/9
1/3	1/3 ⟍ C	BC	1/9
	1/3 — A	CA	1/9
C 1/3 — B	CB	1/9
	1/3 ⟍ C	CC	1/9

Figure 4.2 *Probability tree diagram*

Consider now both bids. The first bid has three possible outcomes and for *each* of these the second has three possible outcomes so that overall there are nine possible outcomes. If we consider any one hotel, for example hotel *A*, only one outcome (*AA*) is favourable to winning both bids. Hence the probability is 1/9 (as we saw above). If we do not specify the hotel and simply find the probability that the *same* hotel wins both bids, then it is clear from Figure 4.2 that there are now three favourable outcomes (*AA, BB* and *CC*). The probability is now 3/9 = 1/3. It is important therefore to specify clearly the probability that is being calculated.

If we consider the hotel chain owning hotels *A* and *B* then we can see from the tree diagram that the probability of its winning both contracts is 4/9 (*AA, AB, BA* and *BB* being the four favourable events out of the nine possible). The probability can also be calculated directly via the multiplication theorem. The probability of winning bid 1 is 2/3 as is the probability of winning bid 2. The probability of winning both bids is hence:

$$P(\text{both bids}) = 2/3 \times 2/3 = 4/9.$$

In the above problem we have implicitly assumed that the two events are independent – that is, the probability of a hotel winning the second contract is unaffected by whether or not it wins the first. If events are not independent then we must allow for this in the calculation of probabilities prior to multiplying them. Suppose, for instance, that the hotels are too small to accommodate both banquets so that winning the first contract disqualifies a hotel from winning the second. What is now the probability of the chain winning both contracts? The first part of the problem remains unchanged – the chain has a 2/3 chance of winning. However, for the second part the chances are changed. *If* one of its hotels has won the first contract, then the chain has only one left to bid for the second contract. Its chances of winning become then 1/2. From the multiplication theorem we have:

$$P(\text{both bids}) = 2/3 \times 1/2 = 2/6 = 1/3.$$

From the tree diagram we can see that this is correct. The number of possible outcomes has been reduced to six (*AA*, *BB* and *CC* are no longer possible). Of these six, two are favourable to the chain (*AB* and *BA*). The probability of the chain winning both bids has thus been slightly reduced.

We can see that in the above case the probability of the second event occurring depends on the outcome of the first. For this reason, the second probability is called a *conditional* probability. We have calculated the probability of the hotel chain winning the second bid as 1/2. However, this is conditional on it winning the first bid. If hotel *C* wins the first bid then either *A* or *B* must win the second and the probability is therefore one. However, this case is irrelevant to the problem under consideration. Clearly the chain cannot win both bids if *C* wins the first one. A conditional probability is denoted as follows:

$$P(\text{bid 2} \mid \text{bid 1}) = 1/2$$

meaning the probability of winning bid 2 *assuming* that bid 1 has been won is 1/2.

Setting the multiplication theorem in a general context, we can say that the probability of two events *A* and *B* both occurring is equal to the probability of *A* occurring multiplied by the probability of *B* occurring assuming that *A* has occurred. That is,

$$P(A \cap B) = P(A) \times P(B \mid A)$$

This formula may be extended to as many consecutive events as required, for instance:

$$P(A \cap B \cap C) = P(A) \times P(B \mid A) \times P(C \mid BA)$$

Students often feel uncomfortable about statistics at this point because it does not provide precise right and wrong type answers. However, a moment's reflection is sufficient to realize that there is no alternative. It is simply not possible to provide precise answers in uncertain or risky situations. All that we can do is calculate the odds and act accordingly. If we do this then we should be correct more often than we are incorrect.

Let us consider one final application of the multiplication theorem. What is the probability that there is a power failure on the same night that the hotel achieves 100% occupancy? Clearly the two probabilities are independent. Suppose we know that the hotel is full (event A) only on 10 occasions each year (and that these occasions are randomly distributed throughout the year) and that power failures (event B) occur once every 2 years. The probability of both occurring at once is then

$$P(A \cap B) = P(A) \times P(B) = 10/365 \times 1/730 = 10/266450 = 1/26645$$

This example demonstrates a number of things. First, the multiplication theorem allows us to identify quickly favourable and total outcomes. As always we could proceed from first principles, but the process would be extremely tiresome. Imagine, for instance, trying to solve this problem using a tree diagram. Event A has 365 possible outcomes and for each of these event B has 730 so that overall we have 266,450 possible outcomes of which 10 are favourable.

Second, given the data available, there is a very low probability that the two events will both occur. However, this does not mean that such an event will not happen. The probability figure tells us that it will occur roughly once every 73 years. In this particular example it would presumably be uneconomic to prepare for such an unlikely event but in other situations preparation may be warranted (e.g. the 50 year wind in house and bridge construction). Of course we may also be unlucky and tonight may be the night that the power failure and 100% occupancy do occur simultaneously.

Third, probability does not tell you *when* events will occur. For instance, the example above should not be interpreted to mean that power failure and 100% occupancy will occur in 73 years time. It means that on the average such as event will occur only once during any 73 year period. You might think that this is not the information that would be of most use (and most people would agree) but it is the best that we can do. Anything else comes into the realm of fortune telling.

Fourth, probability is calculated with respect to the future. You should try to avoid making the common error known as the maturity of chances. To demonstrate what this means, let us take our example a little further. What is the probability of getting a power failure and 100% occupancy two days running? If we define event A as being that we get this result one night and event B that we get it again the following night then the probability of both occurring is found in the usual way. We shall assume for the sake of argument that the two events are independent giving:

$$P(A \cap B) = P(A) \times P(B) = 1/26645 \times 1/26645 = 1/709956025$$

Notice that although the probability is extremely low, it is not zero. There remains a chance that this event will occur – roughly once every 2 million years. For practical purposes we may treat such a probability as zero but this regrettably does not make it zero. If the consequences of being incorrect are not catastrophic then not much harm is likely to be done. In certain circumstances, however, treating low probabilities as if they were zero may not be justified (e.g. where the extinction of animal species might result).

Now suppose that the unlikely does indeed happen and that one night we have 100% occupancy and a power failure occurs. What is the probability that we get the second night also? Those who believe in the maturity of chances will argue that it is next to impossible for this to happen. However, probability looks only forward. Once the event has occurred the probability of it occurring again is back to 1/26645. Thus although it remains unlikely to occur again, once the first event has occurred the odds are nothing like as bad as they might appear initially.

The reasoning may become clearer if we use a simple example with which you can experiment yourselves. What is the probability of getting four heads if we flip a penny four times? Define events A, B, C, and D as being heads on the first, second, third and fourth throws. Then we have

$$P(A) = P(B) = P(C) = P(D) = 1/2$$

and

$$P(A \cap B \cap C \cap D) = P(A) \times P(B) \times P(C) \times P(D) = 1/16$$

Hence if you keep tossing a coin four times and noting the outcomes, then only one set of four throws in every 16 sets should have four heads (on the average). Suppose however that you have already thrown 3 heads, what is the probability of getting a fourth? The answer is 1/2 and not 1/16. You can easily verify this, if you have sufficient patience (and stamina). Make a special note of those occasions when you get heads on each of the first three throws. You should find that roughly half the time you get the fourth head to complete the set. The reason is simple. The probability is one half because the coin has no memory. If, in common with those who believe in the maturity of chances, you try to impute intelligence to coins, cards or roulette wheels you would be well advised not to gamble!

The source of probability estimates

So far we have assumed either that the probabilities of events were known or that all events were equally likely. Where, however, are we to get the probability figures in practice? Three basic sources suggest themselves. First, in some situations it may be possible to deduce probabilities directly. For instance, the probability of rolling one with an unbiased die is 1/6. As we said at the beginning of the chapter, statisticians often use games to illustrate the principles of the subject precisely because the probabilities may be deduced in this way.

Second, some situations may be totally uncertain so that no objective probability estimates may be made. For instance, what is the probability that the USSR will declare war on the USA in 2190. The information simply does not exist to make an objective decision about the probability of this. All that can be done then is to make a guess. If we then use this guess in probability calculations, it is called a subjective probability. Where firms are faced with an uncertain situation requiring a subjective probability it is common practice to use one or more consultants knowledgeable about the particular area and then to proceed on the basis of their opinion. The so-called Delphi method is a more sophisticated version of this. Whatever method is used to arrive at a probability figure, it should always be borne in mind that it is essentially a guess. Not too much should therefore be made of the precise probability calculations that emerge using it.

Third, most business situations enable the use to be made of empirical probabilities, which fall between the two extremes mentioned above. Either we examine past records of the company to establish the frequency with which different events occur. For instance, the figures on 100% occupancy used above would come in practice from past records. All kinds of probability data can be gleaned from company records provided these are accurately kept. Or we can conduct experiments to try to determine the probabilities of different events. For instance, we might deliberately vary the prices of different items to deduce the probability of an increase in sales sufficient to increase turnover.

Conclusion

Having considered the basic ideas underlying probability, we can go on to apply them to business problems. To do this we will develop the idea of the probability distribution. It is important, however, that you keep in mind that all of probability theory is constructed around the fairly elementary ideas presented in this chapter.

Before we look at probability distributions and apply them to particular data sets, we need to consider where the data set itself is to come from. It is to this issue that we turn in the next chapter.

References

A very useful primer on probability with some interesting problems is:

HUFF, D. (1986), *How to Take a Chance*, Pelican.

An application of basic probability theory to an interesting problem facing the hospitality industry is presented in:

CORNEY, W. (1984), 'The use of computer spreadsheets for overbooking optimization and analysis', *International Journal of Hospitality Management*, **3 (4)**: 153–157.

See also:

GULLEN, H. and RHODES, G. (1983), *Management in the Hotel and Catering Industry*, Batsford, chapter 10.

Exercises

1 Using the data presented in Exercise 2 following Chapter 3, find the following probabilities:
   (a) if one person is chosen at random the probability that he or she is a non-union member earning £15,000 or more;
   (b) if one person is chosen at random, the probability that he or she earns less than £12,000 or is a union member;
   (c) if a random sample of 5 people is taken without replacement, the probability that all 5 are union members;
   (d) if a random sample of 3 people is taken without replacement, the probability that one of them earns less than £10,000;

(e) if a random sample of 3 people is taken without replacement, the probability that at least one of them earns less than £10,000.

2   A hotel bar is in the process of re-stocking. It has re-ordered some wine, beer and spirits from 3 suppliers. It is known from experience that the probabilities that the orders will be delivered on time are respectively 0.8, 0.9 and 0.7. Find the probability that:

(a) all three are delivered on time;
(b) none is on time;
(c) at least one is on time.

5
The problems of samples and questionnaires

This chapter is somewhat different to the others. To begin with, there are very few equations in it. Second, it is rather general because the subject matter is vast and the number of potential situations is infinite. This lack of mathematical sophistication together with the generality sometimes inculcates the feeling that the subject is a bit 'waffly' and not very important. This is a big mistake. Data sets do not just happen – they are the result of decisions to collect particular items of information (and *not* to collect others), in a particular way, over a particular time period. These decisions are absolutely vital to the success or failure of any statistical analysis since, as is perhaps obvious, the validity of such analysis will depend on the kind, quality and quantity of data available.

So far we have tended to assume that the data to be analysed are available to us as if by magic. This assumption seems to be common in statistics texts: indeed many of them, at least in the social sciences, do not even consider problems of data collection, concentrating instead on data analysis. In fact, however, deciding what to collect, collecting, compiling and verifying the data set are probably the most important aspects of any statistical study. They are almost always the most time-consuming elements of a study because the availability and power of relatively inexpensive micro-computers mean that much of the data analysis can be undertaken extremely rapidly. If the basic data set is full of errors or is simply inappropriate to the question being studied, the analysis based upon it will be worthless and may lead to expensive policy errors being made.

Data are generally available from a number of sources. This chapter concentrates mainly on the situation where the company must obtain the data for itself, for example directly from its customers. One method frequently used in such cases is the questionnaire. The problems encountered in the design and analysis of these are also discussed.

Possible data sources

One important data source for any company is its own records. Once a company has been running for a number of years, all kinds of factual information should be available. If the company has a computerized database then it may be possible to analyse this data quite easily. Such data is extremely valuable since it relates to the actual operation of the enterprise – it does not rely on customers answering hypothetical questions concerning how they would react if such-and-such were the case. The kind of data available in this way would include things such as occupancy levels at different times of the year, the effect on bar takings of different kinds of special event, regular customers, energy consumption and so on.

Despite its utility, this data source also has its limits. First, certain kinds of data are unlikely to be present – for instance, were guests satisfied with their stay, how often do they use a hotel during the year, what prices were other suppliers quoting compared to the one chosen, why did certain potential customers choose *not* to use the services offered. In other words, the database is likely to give a good factual picture of what has happened but not of how this was received nor what were the alternatives. A second problem that often arises is that only recent data are easily obtainable. The remainder may be archived in all kinds of ways – floppy disks, tape backups, computer printouts or simply as the original documents. If they exist at all, these archives may well be incomplete. In such cases, a substantial amount of work may be required rebuilding the database before any kind of analysis can begin. Given the almost universal use of computers and the low cost of computerized data storage, it would seem to be in a company's interest to maintain an accurate database even if infrequent use is made of it.

A second common source of data is published material. Much of this comes from various government departments. Data are available concerning all kinds of variable that may be of interest in a particular study – for example, population broken down by age group and region, income, employment, and so on. As well as being printed, this kind of data set is increasingly available in a computerized form, either via a telephone link or on floppy disk. Such data may be very useful when a study is being undertaken. Their main drawback, apart from the cost of some of the data, tends to be the lack of control over variable definition. We are forced to use, for example, the regions defined for the collating of the data (unless very disaggregated data can be obtained). Sometimes this may not matter – the definition used may be sufficiently close to what is required. On other occasions, however, the definition of the variable may be too far removed from what we require for the data to be useful. It is thus extremely important to check precisely how different variables have been defined before using the data.

Official data suffer one or two other drawbacks. First, they may only be available with a longish time lag. In many business situations, we often need data on the situation now. In such cases, much official data will not be too useful since the compilation this year of last year's data often represents a good performance by the data-gathering agency. Second, much official data is subject to correction and revision so that more recent data may not be especially *accurate* – look for example at the balance of payments figures, especially for service items.

A third important data source may be newspapers. Certain data are reported regularly so that it is quite easy to develop and maintain a data set. Items that may be particularly relevant to the hotel and catering industry include the weather, foreign exchange rates, and the stock exchange. All quality newspapers carry detailed data concerning these items on a daily basis.

Despite the availability of data through the sources indicated above, in many situations the company will have to generate its own data set if it wishes to analyse a particular question. This data generation frequently involves the use of surveys and hence inevitably the use of samples.

The remainder of this chapter is concerned with the problem of surveys and sampling. However, let us note once again that in practice, before involving the company in expense of surveying, always check that the necessary data (or something sufficiently close) are not already available.

The value of sampling

The purpose of taking a sample is straightforward. We have a statistical population. By taking a representative subset (sample) of this population, we wish to obtain a reliable image of the population without having to contact all of its members.

The precise definition of the population will depend on the case under consideration. Note however that it is a statistical population that we are talking about – it does not have to contain people. For example, suppose that a company produces prepacked meals for airline passengers. Each tray is supposed to contain in addition to food, etc, a packet containing a plastic knife, fork and spoon. Despite quality control checks, the company has received an unusually high number of complaints that these packets have been missing. It decides, therefore, to implement a more intensive control of the production line over a 2-week period. The population in this case is the number of trays of food produced over the 2-week period.

Suppose that the production line produces meals at the rate of 6 per minute. It is neither economically desirable nor necessary to check every single tray produced. Instead a representative sample of trays should be chosen so that the results obtained in this sample are indicative of what is happening in the population. The difficulty is deciding precisely how to choose this sample. We will return to this issue shortly. Before doing so we will briefly discuss the merits of a sampling approach to this kind of problem.

The major advantage of a sampling approach is one of cost. Examining all members of a population may be an extremely expensive operation, depending of course on the population under consideration. Taking a sample reduces cost substantially and produces similar results, *provided* that the sample is not biased.

In some situations, sampling is the only alternative available. This is so where the item being tested is destroyed in the process. Consider, for instance, wine tasting. If a sampling approach were not used, no saleable product would remain. Sampling is also unavoidable where the population is effectively infinite. Imagine for example the situation faced by an international organization that wishes to assess the impact of an advertising campaign designed to increase consumer awareness world-wide. There is clearly no economically feasible way by which all potential customers may be contacted and so a sample will have to be taken.

Finally, data can usually be generated and analysed more quickly in the case of a sample than in the case of the entire population (at least for a given cost level). This speed has a number of advantages. First, decisions, may be taken more rapidly. Second, within the sample the problem of time-based variation can be eliminated. A survey based on the population may take so long to complete that answers vary not only, for example, according to the region but also according to the time of year (month, day, etc.). Lastly, since the sample is smaller it is more easily controlled so that the quality of the data available tends to be better.

Types of sampling

Random sampling

Statistical methods are based almost exclusively on the idea of *random sampling* – that is to say a sample where every member of the population has an equal chance of being included. In practice, generating a genuinely random sample can be extremely difficult. It may also result in a sample that is impractical and/or expensive to contact.

Let us begin with the most straightforward situation. If it is possible to identify each member of the population, they can each be assigned a number and a random sample is easily constructed by drawing these numbers at random (either by using random number tables – see Murdoch and Barnes, Table 24, p. 30 – or by generating random numbers using a computer).

Some situations lend themselves to this approach. The example above concerning the trays of food is a case in point. We know that trays are produced at the rate of 6 per minute. Assuming that the company operates an 8-hour day 5-day week, this means that (about) 28,800 trays will be produced over the 2-week control period. We can number these from 1 to 28,800 (conceptually only, we do not actually have to label each tray with a number). Suppose that it is decided to test 20% of trays then we simply draw 5760 numbers at random and these identify which trays are to be tested as they emerge from the production line. We would need to count the trays as they appear.

The basis from which the sample is drawn is called the *sampling frame*. ✓ Often the identification of this frame is a tricky problem. It is common to find studies which begin with a *frame survey*, the main objective of which is to enumerate all members of the population thereby establishing the sampling frame.

Often in service industries, sampling involves human populations. In such cases the establishment of the appropriate sampling frame may be especially difficult. The clearest situation will be one where customers using the establishment over a given period, say the past year, are sampled. Here provided records have been accurately kept, the sampling frame is easily established. A sample may then be drawn up and customers contacted.

In many situations, however, the relevant sample is not so much actual customers as potential customers. Here, a sampling frame is next to impossible to set up and bias may easily creep into the sample unless it is very carefully designed. For example, suppose that a restaurant is surveying its customers as to those features that made them choose it. While some useful information may be generated in this way, it may be even more relevant from a managerial viewpoint to consider those who are rejecting the present image than those who are accepting it. It is, of course, much easier (and more pleasant) to generate a sample of people who are happy with the facilities than it is those who are not. Consequently, the sample may easily be biased into giving an impression that the restaurant is presently providing the features that potential customers want.

Generating a genuinely random sample is not really feasible in the above kind of situation. On the other hand, some careful thought must be given to the design of the survey and the selection of the sample to avoid bias, so far as possible. This may involve nothing more than a simple decision rule to interview at least a certain proportion of potential customers who look at the facilities on offer and decide against them.

One situation where bias is easily introduced into the sample is where the sample selects itself. This situation is frequently encountered in the hospitality industry. For example, many hotels leave comment cards in guests rooms. It is easy to understand that certain kinds of guests are much more likely to respond than others so that there is almost no chance of obtaining a representative sample. If the hotel is offering these cards simply as a means of placating irate guests then this may not matter much. If, however, the intention is to generate some useful information concerning the performance of the hotel then the results are unlikely to be very reliable. It would be far better to organize a correctly designed survey. Most people will participate in such an event if asked, particularly if some small reward is offered for their time (e.g. a drink or meal voucher depending on the importance of the survey). At least in this way the results generated can be analysed using statistical methods and management decisions taken upon the data will have a calculable chance of success.

Systematic random sampling

In certain situations, simple random sampling may not be the most appropriate method. One alternative that is often used is systematic random sampling. This method works well provided that the population is itself randomly distributed.

The basic principle is straightforward. Rather than choosing the entire sample at random, we choose only the first element at random. The remainder are related systematically to this element. For instance, in the example of prepacked airline trays, it was decided to sample 20% of trays – that is, 1 in 5. We choose the first tray at random (from 1 to 5) and take every fifth tray from then onwards.

This method simplifies the task of identifying the sample. It also simplifies the fieldwork in situations where the sampled units arrive sequentially and some time is required with each unit as is the case in the above example. A number of situations are like this. For instance, suppose that a hotel wishes to interview guests as they arrive as to their first impressions of the hotel. Suppose it is decided to interview 10% of guests daily. If we identify these using simple random methods, we may end up choosing to interview the second, third and fourth arrivals.

However, since these may well arrive together, we would have to ask some of them to wait while others are interviewed. This is unlikely to improve first impressions of the hotel. The systematic alternative is to take every tenth guest.

Stratified sampling

Random sampling (simple or systematic) is generally the best method when nothing is known about the population. Where however some information is available, for example from a frame survey, concerning the population, better results can generally be obtained if this information is used to stratify the population (i.e. break it into groups) and then sample according to these groups. Stratification may be applied in all kinds of way reflecting the heterogeneity of the population – sex, age, region, type of business (e.g. business traveller vs. tourist) and so on.

The use of stratified sampling often improves the results obtained from a survey. This is especially so where contacting sampled units is expensive so that the sample is kept small. A small random sample may easily be biased. For example, suppose a hotel has 100 guests, 70 of whom are men and 30 women. If a sample of 10 people is chosen at random, then it may well contain 10 women in which case it could hardly claim to be representative. The stratified alternative would be to choose at random 7 men and 3 women. In this way, knowledge of the population is used to remove as much potential bias as possible. The resulting sample may still be biased (e.g. we may have the youngest 10 people) but we can do no better than to use stratification where we have knowledge and random methods where we do not.

The results of stratification may be improved further if something is known of the variability of the different strata. For instance, suppose that we know that the opinions of businessmen about the quality of service are much more volatile than those of tourists. We would need to interview relatively more businessmen than tourists if we are to get an overall opinion that is representative of both groups. Note, however, that the amount of improvement in the final results will only be substantial if the difference between variances is large.

It should be noted that the value of stratification depends entirely on the accuracy of our knowledge concerning the population. If we have no idea about the structure of the population, it makes little sense to try to stratify. In fact, where there is no sound basis for stratification, it will prove worse than a simple random sample since it will tend to confirm preconceptions regarding the population.

Sampling with probability proportionate to size

Suppose that a hotel chain wishes to take a random sample of 100 guests from its 33 hotels around the country. If we merely stratify by hotel and then take the sample we will end up with very few values per stratum. This may or may not be satisfactory. If however we wish to have a reasonably-sized sample at each level, one method would be to sample according to size.

Consider the four largest hotels in the chain. Suppose hotel A has 500 guests, hotel B 200, hotel C 200 and hotel D 100. In total we have 1000 guests of whom 100 are to be interviewed. Equal probability requires that each guest have a 1/10 chance of being selected.

Suppose, however, that, to keep the cost of the survey down, it is decided to choose one of the four hotels at random and then to interview 100 guests chosen at random in the hotel. How should we select the hotel? If we simply choose it at random then each hotel has 1 chance in 4 of being selected. However, the probabilities at the guest level are incorrect. For example, if hotel 1 is selected, each guest at this hotel then has a 100/500 (= 1/5) chance of being interviewed. We know from probability theory (Chapter 4) that the chance of two independent events occurring is given by the multiplication theorem. Considering the whole study, the probability of a guest at hotel 1 being interviewed is given by the probability that the hotel is chosen (event A) multiplied by the probability that the guest is then chosen (event B), that is:

$$P(A \cap B) = P(A) \times P(B) = 1/4 \times 1/5 = 1/20$$

Taking now hotel 4, if it is selected then each guest is certain to be interviewed (100/100) which gives a probability of:

$$P(A \cap B) = 1/4 \times 1/1 = 1/4$$

If therefore we choose the hotels at random, we bias the selection of the guests – those staying at the largest hotels are less likely to be interviewed.

To ensure that each guest has an equal chance of being interviewed we must sample according to size – that is, each hotel's chance of being selected should be proportionate to the number of guests staying there. This may be achieved by assigning numbers to each hotel in proportion to its number of guests – i.e. hotel 1 has half the guests so it gets 5 numbers out of 10 and so on. This gives the situation shown in Table 5.1.

Table 5.1 *Sampling with probability proportionate to size*

Hotel	No. of guests	Random numbers
1	500	0–4
2	200	5–6
3	200	7–8
4	100	9

The hotel is then selected on the basis of a number drawn at random. If the number selected is between 0 and 4 inclusive, then hotel 1 is chosen; 5 or 6 hotel 2, and so on. It makes no difference how the random numbers are assigned to the hotels.

By deliberately biasing the choice of hotel, we are able to compensate for the size difference and ensure that each guest has an equal chance of being selected. The probability of a guest being interviewed at each of the four hotels is as follows:

$$P(\text{Hotel 1}) = 5/10 \times 100/500 = 1/10$$
$$P(\text{Hotel 2}) = 2/10 \times 100/200 = 1/10$$
$$P(\text{Hotel 3}) = 2/10 \times 100/200 = 1/10$$
$$P(\text{Hotel 4}) = 1/10 \times 100/100 = 1/10$$

Now regardless of the hotel where they are staying, each guest has the same (1/10) chance of being interviewed, and the hotel chain avoids the expense of having to conduct the survey in more than one hotel. Note however that this technique assumes that guests are randomly distributed amongst the hotels. If there is reason to believe otherwise then the technique should be combined with the appropriate stratification.

Problems of questionnaire design and analysis

Frequently surveys are carried out using questionnaires. In this section, we will look at some of the methods that might be used and the difficulties that may be encountered with this approach.

Essentially two methods are available. First, the postal approach (or a version thereof) may be used where the questionnaire is sent to the individual who is asked to complete it on his/her own. Second, an interview approach can be used where a fieldworker completes the questionnaire either with the individual or on the basis of his/her answers.

The principal advantage of the first method is one of cost – many more people can be contacted by post than in situations where face to face interviews are required. In many cases however this advantage is out-weighed by the fact that response rates to postal questionnaires tend to be very low. This is particularly the case where the individual concerned can see no immediate benefit to co-operation. A decision to use a postal approach should only be taken therefore if individuals can be persuaded of the benefit of completing the questionnaire or if some pressure can be exerted on them. Thus if you are conducting a survey among the employees of a hotel chain, a postal approach will probably work whereas if the survey concerns the hotels' customers such an approach will probably produce few results. A low response rate has the added problem that the sample effectively selects itself resulting generally in bias which is difficult to quantify. In most situations where question-naires are used, an interview approach will produce better quality data and it is assumed in the remainder of this section that this approach has been adopted.

One important aspect of conducting an interview-based survey con-cerns the training of field workers. If you are carrying out the survey yourself then there should be no difficulty (other than to ensure that you are consistent in the way that you ask questions). However, in larger surveys staff are often employed to carry out the survey. They must be instructed as to how to ask questions, whether to lead the respondent and if so when, how to interpret particular answers and so on. The quality of data that you eventually acquire will depend critically on your survey team. If they are well trained then a reasonable data set can probably be constructed. If not, you may well find that the data are inconsistent and difficult to interpret. Obviously it is impossible to think in advance of every eventuality that might arise, and this is an important reason for conducting a small-scale pilot study prior to the real thing so that at least frequently-occurring problems can be identified and resolved.

Once the survey is under way, it is important also that someone control the activities of the field staff – both to deal with any queries that arise and to ensure that the survey is being conducted as intended. This control may occur either via data analysis (staff with an unusual pattern of responses can be followed up) or directly in the field by supervisors. Generally, both methods have to be used to ensure good quality consis-tent data. The data analysis has to be contemporaneous – there is clearly no possibility of resolving problems if you wait three months before even looking at the data that has been collected. At the same time, it is unwise to carry out your study at the same time as the data arrive. What must be done therefore is either to select certain questions as a control and check the answers obtained, or to analyse a limited number of complete questionnaires per fieldworker. If controls such as this are not carried out, it is a regrettable but not infrequent experience to find that part of your data set has been generated from the imagination of a fieldworker who was sitting in the local cafe, etc! Such control is even more critical in a large-scale study where fieldworkers may change region over time. In this case, unless control is very tight it will be impossible at the end of the study to separate variations in the data due to the region, time of year (month, day), and fieldworker. In such cases, what appears to be an important seasonal effect may be nothing more than changes in the fieldworkers. Similarly, what appear to be changes related to changes in the fieldworkers may actually be important changes in the variables under study due to season or area. In either case, your study would hardly have been useful to management.

Clearly the best results will arise when as many elements are under your control as possible so that the source of variations can be identified. For instance, all questionnaires should be completed in as little time as possible to eliminate time variations (if you are actually studying time variations, you will need to have different sets of questionnaires at different times – but each set should be completed quickly). At the same time the number of fieldworkers should not be too large so that variation due to fieldworker is minimized. Unfortunately these two criteria conflict – a quick study is likely to require many staff, few staff may require much time. A compromise is required. The one that you choose depends on the study being undertaken. It will also depend on the constraints (budgetary for instance) under which your study is operating. For example, management may decide that a certain number of trainees can be assigned to your study for two weeks each. In this case, it is up to you to design your study around the resources that you have available.

Whether a postal or interview approach is used, at some point a questionnaire will have to be designed. The issues to be investigated must be defined precisely. Decisions must be taken concerning which questions to include and exclude, and how to phrase them. Some thought should also be given at the beginning to the way in which data will be analysed to ensure that, assuming things go as planned, the questionnaire is capable of providing answers to the issues being studied. In questionnaire design, while it is impossible to establish hard and fast rules, there are nonetheless some guidelines that may be enunciated.

First, only ask questions relating to the subject under consideration. It is always tempting when writing a questionnaire to add just one more 'interesting' question. At the same time, make sure that you ask all the questions that you need in order to reach a conclusion on the topic under study. Due to the expense of carrying out questionnaire-based studies, you will probably not have a second chance. Forgetting some vital piece of information may render the whole study worthless. Establishing at the outset exactly what you intend to do with your data and how you are going to analyse them should reduce the risk of missing a crucial element.

Second, in most cases a computer will be used to collate and analyse the data. This means that you will need to consider how you are going to codify the answers that you receive. The precise codes used make little difference so long as it is clear how each answer should be coded. A code must always be designated to identify missing values – i.e. non-response. Take care if you decide to use zero as this code since it often becomes difficult to separate values. which are really zero from those which are missing. Obviously this is disastrous for subsequent data analysis. Since in business situations it is rare to find variables that take negative values, the use of -1 as the missing-value code is recommended.

Third, try to avoid open-ended questions. Obviously this is not always possible and the information that they convey may be extremely interesting. The difficulty comes when you try to analyse them. It is better if possible to try to anticipate the likely answers (perhaps via a pilot study) so as to structure the responses received. At the same time, however, care must be taken not to lead the interviewee.

Fourth, wherever possible ask questions to which the interviewee can provide factual answers. The analysis is then one of drawing inferences from these facts, rather than trying to interpret what the answer might mean. Many of the question cards that one finds scattered around hotel rooms are worse than useless. For instance, what is one to make of a hotel that asks you to rank its service on a scale of 1 to 5? It is immediately apparent that nothing can be inferred from the answers given since such a ranking depends on a mixture of the expectations of the guest and the service actually provided. The service may have been below that aimed for by management yet perceived as satisfactory by the customer. Similarly, the service may have been perfectly adequate given the standards set by management, yet judged inadequate by a particularly grumpy guest. It is far better, if not always possible, to define a level of satisfactory service and then check whether it is being achieved. For instance, how long did you have to wait between ordering breakfast and it being served? (Once again, it is assumed that there is an intention to analyse and learn from the responses. Where the purpose of the card is simply to give the guest the impression that the hotel cares, it obviously does not matter much how the questions are phrased.)

Fifth, in your analysis of the questionnaires you must be organized. Unless the data are correctly coded and entered into the computer, no analysis of them will be particularly worth while. First of all, give each questionnaire a number. This will enable you to ensure that each questionnaire has been entered into the computer, and equally important that no questionnaire has been entered twice. Once the questionnaire has been coded, data entry can be undertaken. Numerous database packages exist: the actual data entry method will depend on the software that you use. The best known package is probably DBase (in its various versions – currently IV). Such packages are generally sufficient for the data entry phase. One difficulty that can occur is where you have a very large questionnaire since there is a limit to the number of variables (fields) that these packages can handle (DBase IV can take up to 250). Where you have more than the limit number, you can either divide your database or write your own data entry routine in a programming language (Pascal, Basic, etc). In any case, even where an off-the-shelf package is used, some programming is likely to be required – for instance, if you wish to control a range of values or if you wish to jump to different variables depending on the values entered. (For example, you may have a question asking which airline company your guests used. Such a question will only have a response if people arrived by plane – hence the question can be jumped in the data entry phase if they arrived some other way and the default value may be left in place).

Actual data analysis will depend on what you wish to achieve. A database package can be used to calculate some statistics, but it is generally better to transfer your data to a dedicated package. Data transfer is fairly straightforward these days provided that you have access to recent versions of software. Most packages provide at least the option to output data in ASCII-format, and once this is done you can import your data into other software.

Coding of answers may either be done directly on the questionnaire or on a separate coding sheet. Data entry is generally faster if you use a coding sheet since the operator does not need to turn the pages on the questionnaire. Moreover, many questionnaires can often be coded on the same sheet.

If coding is done directly on the questionnaire it is fairly frequent to find a column left for this purpose. This is not essential however. All that is required is some method of drawing the operator's eye to the correct place for data entry. A red pen is usually sufficient – either underlining the values that must be entered or writing them out. Leaving a column separates the data entry from the remainder but may necessitate much copying of obvious data. It may also give the questionnaire an undesirably official look from the point of view of the respondent.

When a coding sheet is used, it generally makes sense to code across the page. The operator may then use a ruler to underline the figures to be entered, moving down the page as each set of data is completed.

Once the data have been entered, they must be checked. The obvious way to do this is to print out the data held by the computer and compare with those on the original questionnaire (not the coding sheet since transcription errors may have occurred, which have been correctly entered into the computer). Once corrections have been made the corrected questionnaire must be checked again (and again) until no errors are found. It is generally worthwhile asking the staff entering the data to staple a correct print-out of the data to the questionnaire, first to ensure that it really is correct and second to enable quick checking of any anomalies found at the data analysis stage.

An alternative method of correcting data is to enter the same data twice either by the same operator or independently by two different operators. The two sets of data are then checked. This checking may easily be done by computer using a spreadsheet. The first set is entered. The second set is then subtracted on a cell-by-cell basis. If the two data sets agree, then we will have zeros all over the spreadsheet. A value different to zero clearly means that the two sets of data disagree, and the originals may be checked simply for such values. Again we go on checking until no errors are found.

Both methods will ensure that the data is eventually correct. They both have their defects. Printing out and checking the data can become extremely tedious and long-winded. On the other hand, entering the same data twice tends to de-motivate data entry staff since they tend to feel that it does not matter too much what they do. Obviously if both people feel like this then the number of errors may increase. Paying a part of salary as a bonus for accurate work may help.

It cannot be overemphasized that time (and money) must be spent to ensure that the data are as accurate as possible. Once the data are entered into the computer and verified, their analysis may commence. The methods used will depend on the problem under consideration.

Conclusion

This chapter has considered the problems involved in obtaining the basic data set which is to be analysed. The major issues considered here are those of sampling and the use of questionnaires. In both cases it is clear that a number of decisions must be taken concerning how to proceed. These decisions will affect the quantity and quality of data available for later analysis. The obvious point bears repetition one last time that if the basic data set is flawed then no matter how sophisticated the analytical methods used no worthwhile results will be obtained. Assuming that accurate data are available, the next chapter returns to the issue of how to analyse them.

References

Two articles that address the problems of samples and particularly questionnaire design are:

MARTIN, W. (1986), 'Defining what quality service is for you', *Cornell HRA Quarterly*, February, pp. 32–38.
MARTIN, W. (1986), 'Measuring and improving your service quality', *Cornell HRA Quarterly*, May, pp. 80–87.

Also of interest is:

LEWIS, R. (1983), 'When guests complain', *Cornell HRA Quarterly*, August, pp. 23–32.

The use of questionnaires in marketing is considered in:

SHEPHERD, J. (1982), *Marketing Practice in the Hotel and Catering Industry*, Batsford, chapter 3, especially pp. 50–58.

Exercises

1   Using one of the unclassified data sets presented in the exercises following Chapter 2, take random samples of 10, 30 and 50 values and calculate the mean for each sample. Assuming that the set of values presented in Chapter 2 comprises the population, compare your sample results with the population mean.
2   Now take the same sample sizes using a systematic approach. How do the results compare?
3   Finally, stratify the population in some way (for example, if you use the data set from the first exercise, break the population into three salary groups) and select the same size samples using random sampling within the different strata. How does this affect your results?

6
The binomial probability distribution

The principal purpose of this chapter is to introduce the idea of a probability distribution by looking at what is probably the most straightforward of these – the binomial. Do not be put off by the jargon; 'binomial' merely means 'two numbers' and a 'probability distribution' is just the set of probabilities for all the possible outcomes to a particular problem or situation.

Before discussing the binomial, it will be useful to develop a little further the issue raised in Chapter 4 of counting the number of outcomes in a probability problem.

Determining the number of outcomes

We saw in Chapter 4 that in a probability problem we can always proceed (in principle anyway) by writing out all the possible solutions and then observing which of these are favourable to our experiment. Clearly, however, this approach becomes less and less feasible as the number of possible outcomes increases. What often surprises is how quickly the numbers increase in this kind of exercise.

Suppose that we are putting together a 3-course menu. We wish to offer our customers a reasonable choice but at the same time we want to keep the menu under control so that it is easy to plan and manage. How many different dishes should we offer at each stage? Let us suppose that we decide to offer the customers a choice of 7 entrees, 4 main courses and 7 sweets. This seems to offer a rather restricted choice to the customer and we may well wish to increase the choice at each level. However, before taking such decisions, let us see how many different meals are possible with the present situation.

One possible approach would be to draw a tree diagram illustrating the above problem. This, however, is left as an exercise for those who enjoy such things. Let us rather try to develop a general principle from the example. Each customer chooses one of seven entrees. For each of these entrees she chooses one of four main meals. There are thus twenty-eight different choices for entree followed by main course. Having chosen one of these twenty-eight, the customer then chooses a dessert from the seven on offer. This means that there are 196 (= 28 × 7) different meals possible with this menu. The number of possible meals increases rather quickly as we add courses or dishes. For instance, simply adding two extra main courses to the menu increases the number of possible meals to 294.

As a general rule then we can say that if a first task has x possible outcomes, and for each of these x a second outcome has y possible outcomes, then task 1 followed by task 2 has $x \times y$ possible outcomes.

Permutations and combinations

Sometimes the problem under consideration falls into the category of permutation or combination, in which case we may use the formulae that exist for evaluating these. Both permutations and combinations relate to sets.

If we have a set of objects then sometimes the order in which they occur matters whereas on other occasions the order is irrelevant. Consider for example a group of people registering for a conference. The order in which they register makes no difference – they will still all be registered for the conference. Hence from this point of view there is just one set of people and the order in which they appear is irrelevant. However, once we come to assigning them to their rooms the way that they are arranged (their order) does matter because obviously assigning Mr A to room 1 and Mr B to room 2 is not the same as assigning Mr A to room 2 and Mr B to room 1. Hence from the point of view of room distribution there is not just one group but many different groups even though the number of people being considered has not changed.

The situation where the order matters is called a *permutation* while the situation where it does not matter is a *combination*. Clearly for a given set of numbers there will be many more permutations than combinations.

Let us look first at the formula for calculating the number of permutations. Take the following simple example. Suppose we have two guests (A and B) and three rooms (1, 2, and 3). How many different allocations of guests to rooms are possible? As was stated above this is a permutation because the order matters – that is, adopting a shorthand notation, (A1 B2) is not the same as (A2 B1) even though the same rooms and the same people are involved. The set of possible outcomes is then as follows:

(A1 B2),(A1 B3), (A2 B1), (A2 B3), (A3 B1) and (A3 B2). Hence there are six possible outcomes.

Consider a general situation where we have *n* objects and we are going to take permutations of size *m*. The number of such permutations is given by the formula:

$$\prescript{n}{m}{P} = \frac{n!}{(n-m)!}$$

where *n*! means *n* factorial. This notation is best explained by means of an example. If we have 5! then this is a shorthand way of writing $5 \times 4 \times 3 \times 2 \times 1$, and 7! means $7 \times 6 \times 5 \times 4 \times 3 \times 2 \times 1$. The only point to note about the factorial notation is that 0! is taken to equal 1 (as is 1!) to avoid dividing by zero.

Returning to our example then we have:

$$\prescript{3}{2}{P} = \frac{3!}{(3-2)!} = \frac{3 \times 2 \times 1}{1} = 6 \text{ (as before)}$$

It is often a source of amazement how quickly the numbers increase in a permutation situation. If we increase the number of available rooms to ten for eight guests then the number of possible allocations of guests to rooms becomes:

$$\prescript{10}{8}{P} = \frac{10!}{(10-8)!} = \frac{10 \times 9 \times 8 \times 7 \times \ldots \times 2 \times 1}{2 \times 1} = 1,814,400$$

Many people find it difficult to believe that such a result can be true. The only practical advice to give is not be to the duty manager on the night that nobody is happy with their room – you could be a long time resolving the problem!

In the case of combinations the numbers involved are somewhat smaller. Suppose that you have two single rooms (1 and 2) left for 3 potential guests (A, B and C). How many different sets of guests are there with a room? This time the order does not matter – whether we give Room 1 to Mr A and Room 2 to Mr B or vice versa they still both have a room. Hence, in the case of combinations, (A1 B2) is the same as (A2 B1). The possible combinations are: [(A1 B2) or (A2 B1)] [(A1 C2) or (A2 C1)] [(B1 C2) or (B2 C1)]. There are thus three of them, but each one can occur in two different ways. As should be apparent, these different ways are the number of permutations. It will come as no surprise therefore that the formula for calculating the number of combinations is closely related to that for permutations. We simply divide the number of permutations by the number of ways in which each combination may occur.

The general formula for calculating the number of combinations is thus:

$$\prescript{n}{}{C}_{m} = \frac{n!}{(n - m)! \times m!}$$

Since the denominator is bound to be larger than in the case of permutations the number of combinations must be less. Continuing the example we have:

$$\prescript{3}{}{C}_{2} = \frac{3!}{(3 - 2)! \times 2!} = \frac{3 \times 2 \times 1}{1 \times 2 \times 1} = 3 \quad \text{(as before)}$$

One thing to notice is that the arithmetic involved in calculating the number of permutations and combinations usually simplifies significantly merely because so much of the problem divides out.

The binomial probability distribution

Having looked at permutations and especially combinations we can move on to consider the binomial probability distribution. As was noted above, the name 'binomial' simply means 'two numbers' and hence the binomial probability distribution applies to problems where there are only two possible outcomes to each event. At first sight this may seem to limit the binomial substantially but in fact there are many situations that are binomial in nature – for instance any yes/no problem.

Consider for a moment a simple example. Suppose that a quality control machine accepts or rejects tins according to their weight. From experience we know that 10% of tins are rejected. We will suppose therefore that the probability of any single tin being rejected is 1/10 and hence the probability that it is accepted is 9/10. If we consider three tins, what is the probability that none, one, two or all three will be rejected. Table 6.1 classifies the possible results by the number of tins rejected (R) and accepted (A).

Table 6.1   *Possible outcomes and probability in a binomial problem*

No. of rejects	Outcomes	Probability
0	AAA	9/10 × 9/10 × 9/10 = 729/1000
1	AAR	9/10 × 9/10 × 1/10 = 81/1000
1	ARA	9/10 × 1/10 × 9/10 = 81/1000
1	RAA	1/10 × 9/10 × 9/10 = 81/1000
2	ARR	9/10 × 1/10 × 1/10 = 9/1000
2	RAR	1/10 × 9/10 × 1/10 = 9/1000
2	RRA	1/10 × 1/10 × 9/10 = 9/1000
3	RRR	1/10 × 1/10 × 1/10 = 1/1000

We can see that there are 8 possible outcomes, each with some chance of occurring. However, if we define an event such as the probability of obtaining one reject then we can see that this may occur in one of three different ways so that:

$$P(R = 1) = 81/1000 + 81/1000 + 81/1000 = 243/1000.$$

Similarly the probability of getting 2 rejects is 27/1000. In the case of the other two events (0 and 3 rejects) there is only one favourable outcome so that the probabilities are given immediately as 729/1000 and 1/1000 respectively.

If we draw up a table of possible outcomes with their probabilities as follows then we have a probability distribution:

$$P(R = 3) = 1/1000 = 0.001$$
$$P(R = 2) = 27/1000 = 0.027$$
$$P(R = 1) = 243/1000 = 0.243$$
$$P(R = 0) = 729/1000 = 0.729$$

Notice that the probabilities sum to one. In other words all outcomes are included – if we consider three tins, one of the above outcomes must occur.

The distribution that we have here is called a binomial probability distribution because it has the following characteristics:

1   There is a fixed number of identical trials. Here three tins are considered.
2   Each trial has only two possible outcomes usually called success and failure, although these terms may be misleading. It is important to note that success and failure are here defined with respect to the event

under consideration. Sometimes this may lead to 'success' not having its usual meaning. In the example above, we are interested in finding the probability that tins will be rejected and thus 'success' is defined as a tin being rejected. Wherever possible, it is a good idea to set up the problem so that the meaning of 'success' and 'failure' emerges intuitively. However, as our example demonstrates this is not necessary. The same kind of point needs to be made concerning 'favourable' and 'unfavourable' outcomes. All of these terms, 'success', 'failure', 'favourable', 'unfavourable', are defined with respect to the problem under consideration and not necessarily with respect to any common-sense definition of success, etc.

3   The probability of success (denoted as p) is known and is constant from one trial to the next. The probability of failure (q) is given as $1 - p$ (since one of the two outcomes must occur on each trial).

4   The outcome of any one trial is independent of the outcome of any other trial.

Rather than having to write out all possible outcomes each time that we encounter a binomial problem, it would be helpful if we could develop a formula-based approach from the basic principles that we have encountered so far. As it happens, a variety of such approaches exists.

First, working from the definitions above, the two possible outcomes of any one trial may be written as:

$$(p + q)$$

i.e. either success or failure must occur with probabilities given by p and q. If we consider two trials then all possible outcomes and their probabilities may be found by multiplying the possible outcomes of each trial, that is:

$$(p + q) \times (p + q) = (p + q)^2$$

If a third trial is added we have

$$(p + q) \times (p + q) \times (p + q) = (p + q)^3$$

and so on.
In general we have

$$(p + q)^n \text{ for } n \text{ trials.}$$

If we expand the brackets for the case of three trials then we obtain:

$$p^3 + 3p^2q + 3pq^2 + q^3$$

Substituting in for the values of p and q from the quality control example, where p is 9/10 and q is 1/10, gives:

$$(9/10)^3 + 3 \times (9/10)^2 \times (1/10) + 3 \times (9/10) \times (1/10)^2 + (1/10)^2$$

which equals

$$729/1000 + 243/1000 + 27/1000 + 1/1000$$

exactly as before.

Alternatively, it can be shown that any particular probability can be found by evaluating Equation (6.1) below for the appropriate value of x. This equation is derived as follows. The expansion of $(p + q)^n$ is given by:

$$\underset{x}{\overset{n}{C}}\ p^x\ q^{n-x} \text{ for } x = 0, 1, 2, \dots\dots , n.$$

Taking for example the case where n is 3, we obtain:

$$(p + q)^3 \; = \; \underset{0}{\overset{3}{C}}\ p^0 q^{3-0} \; + \; \underset{1}{\overset{3}{C}}\ p^1 q^{3-1} \; + \; \underset{2}{\overset{3}{C}}\ p^2 q^{3-2} \; + \; \underset{3}{\overset{3}{C}}\ p^3 q^{3-3}$$

$$= \frac{3!}{0! \times 3!}\ (1)\ q^3 + \frac{3!}{1! \times 2!}\ p\, q^2 + \frac{3!}{2! \times 1!}\ p^2\, q + \frac{3!}{3! \times 0!}\ p^3 \quad (1)$$

$$= \frac{3 \times 2 \times 1}{1 \times 3 \times 2 \times 1}\ q^3 + \frac{3 \times 2 \times 1}{1 \times 2 \times 1}\ p\, q^2 + \frac{3 \times 2 \times 1}{2 \times 1 \times 1}\ p^2\, q + \frac{3 \times 2 \times 1}{3 \times 2 \times 1 \times 1}\ p^3$$

$$= q^3 + 3pq^2 + 3p^2q + p^3 \quad \text{(as before).}$$

Although this looks quite complicated at first, it means that any particular probability in a binomial problem may be found using Equation 6.1:

$$P(x) = \underset{x}{\overset{n}{C}}\ p^x\ q^{n-x} \; \dots\dots \tag{6.1}$$

In the quality control example, we have as our basic parameters $n = 3$, $p = 9/10$ and $q = 1/10$. To find, for instance, the probability of getting 2 rejects, we must evaluate Equation 6.1 using these values for n, p and q and with x set equal to 2. This gives:

$$P(R=2) = \underset{2}{\overset{3}{C}} \ (9/10)^2 \ (1/10)^1 = \frac{3 \times 2 \times 1}{2 \times 1 \times 1} \ (.81)(.1) = 3 \ (.81)(.1)$$

$$= .243 \quad \text{(precisely as before)}$$

To reinforce the ideas developed so far we will discuss one further example.

From inspection of its past records a hotel finds that its average carry over is 20%. If 10 guests are registered for a particular night what is the probability that none will wish to stay on (i.e. that the carry over will be zero).

Before we calculate this let us briefly mention one common approach to the carry over problem and to other management problems. This is what might be called 'management by averages'. Since there are ten guests registered and the average carry over is 20%, most people will realize that the most likely outcome is for 2 guests to stay on. However simply because this is the most likely *individual* outcome does not mean that it necessarily makes good managerial sense to act as if it were the only thing that could happen.

Let us consider the likelihood of no one staying on. Notice first that this can be treated as a binomial problem since each guest either stays on or not. The probability may not in practice remain constant from trial to trial, but we have no way of assigning individual probabilities to guests so that using the empirically-determined probability is probably the best we can do. There may also be some interdependence between guests – e.g. couples, parties, etc. – and this would have to be allowed for. Assuming independence however gives the following results.

We need to begin by identifying the key values in the binomial distribution. From the data on average carry over we can say that the probability of any one person staying on (success in this case) is 0.2. Therefore the probability of failure, q, (they do not stay) must be 0.8. We know that n is 10. Define X as the number of guests who stay on, then we must evaluate the following:

$$P(X=0) = \underset{0}{\overset{10}{C}} \ 0.2^0 0.8^{10-0}$$

$$= 0.8^{10} = 0.1074$$

In other words there is about an 11% chance that there will be no carry over. Hence if the hotel were to adopt a strict strategy of reserving 2 rooms for the expected carry over then about 11% of the time it would be left with these two rooms unsold.

Other probabilities may be found in similar fashion. The probability of there being only one carry over is:

$$P(X=1) = \begin{matrix}10\\C\\1\end{matrix}\ 0.2^{1} \cdot 0.8^{10-1}$$

$$= 10 \times 0.2 \times .13422 = 0.26844$$

Hence about 27% of the time one of the rooms would be unsold. In total the hotel would be left with free rooms about 38% of the time. Of course the strategy being suggested is very naive and hotels would quickly learn that it did not payoff. However it is interesting that managing on the basis of averages should give such poor results. We can calculate the percentage of time that the strategy would work exactly as follows:

$$P(X=2) = \begin{matrix}10\\C\\2\end{matrix}\ 0.2^{2} \cdot 0.8^{10-2}$$

$$= 45 \times .04 \times .16777 = .302$$

Thus only about 30% of the time would the hotel have set aside the correct number of rooms (that is to say, the most likely single outcome occurs only 30% of the time). Since the hotel has undersold about 38% of the time and got it right about 30% of the time, then in about 32% (i.e. the remainder) of cases the hotel will have oversold. Such doublebooking is commonplace in some countries' hotel industries, although in many places it is actually illegal. It may have serious consequences for the hotel. Basing a management strategy only on average values is clearly not to be recommended. Consideration must also be given to the likely spread of values around this average (that is, to the probability distribution) and to the costs and benefits of different strategies.

Whenever we are faced with a binomial problem, the probabilities of different events may be calculated using Equation (6.1). Sometimes, however, the form of the problem will be a little different from that given as an example above so that, although the formula remains the same, its use will require some small modification.

For instance, suppose that the hotel manager asks you to calculate the probability that more than 2 guests stay on in the situation above. Equation 6.1 only enables us to calculate the probabilities of specific events (e.g. $P(X=2)$). However here we want $P(X>2)$. This calculation may be written as:

$$P(X>2) = P(X=3)+P(X=4)+P(X=5)+$$
$$P(X=6)+P(X=7)+P(X=8)+P(X=9)+P(X=10)$$

Clearly performing this calculation would be very time-consuming. It may be possible to simplify matters by using the rule that the sum of probabilities must equal one (provided that all possible outcomes are included). This gives:

$$P(X=0)+P(X=1)+P(X=2)+P(X=3)+P(X=4)+P(X=5)+$$
$$P(X=6)+P(X=7)+P(X=8)+P(X=9)+P(X=10) = 1$$

Rearranging slightly gives:

$$1 - \{P(X=0)+P(X=1)+P(X=2)\} = P(X=3)+P(X=4)+$$
$$P(X=5)+P(X=6)+P(X=7)+P(X=8)+P(X=9)+P(X=10)$$

Thus rather than calculating the 8 probabilities on the right-hand side of the equation, we can calculate the three on the left-hand side and obtain the same answer. This method of rearranging a problem was introduced in Chapter 4. It often pays off in probability and is well worth remembering.

However, although the rearrangement shown above works well here, it is clear that if the number of guests were increased to 200 the calculations would become practically impossible. There are a number of ways out of this dilemma.

First, we could use binomial probability tables (see Murdoch and Barnes, Table 1). The tables give the probability that X will exceed a particular value, given the values of n and p. Only certain values of n and p are given, for practical reasons (the number of possible pairs of values is limitless) and also because other probability distributions can often be used to give a good approximation to the binomial (see below and next chapter). Note that, as the tables give $P(X \geqslant x)$, to find, for example, $P(X=2)$ you must find $P(X \geqslant 2) - P(X \geqslant 3)$.

Second, we could use the calculating power of a computer. It is not difficult to program the computer to solve the problem. A BASIC program listing is included as an appendix to this chapter. The program is structured as follows. Lines 10–80 set up the initial values for n and p (and hence q). Some error traps are included – it is not possible to enter a nonsense value for probability or the number of trials. Once the initial data has been entered, the program goes to the menu of options (lines 170–300). At present only four options exist (including one to change the values of n and p, and one to exit the program) but you could easily add others if you wish. The program will calculate the probability that X equals a given value (option B – lines 400–500) and the probability that it is greater than a given value (option C – lines 510–660). Each of these options uses the subroutine contained in lines 90–160 which calculates the probability that X equals a particular value. This subroutine only works for values of n up to about 125. Beyond this point, the value of the variable P5 in line 100 may become too small for the computer and be set to zero. Developing the program to handle this problem is possible but would be of limited value since, as we shall see in the next chapter, the normal approximation to the binomial provides very good results once n goes beyond 100. This is why most binomial tables provide probabilities only for values of n up to 100. The program here will produce all the probabilities found in a set of standard tables (e.g. Murdoch and Barnes) in addition to providing the missing values. For instance, using the tables to solve a problem with $p = 0.4256$ and $n = 23$ requires that you interpolate between tabulated values whereas the program will calculate the answer exactly.

Third, where the value of n is reasonably large (around 30), answers to binomial probability problems can be found with what is usually sufficient accuracy by using the normal probability distribution instead. It is easier to use this distribution for calculation purposes as tables exist for all possible values (e.g. Murdoch and Barnes, Tables 3, 4 and 5). The next chapter discusses the use of this distribution.

Conclusion

The purpose of this chapter was to introduce the idea of a probability distribution using as an example the binomial. As we have seen this distribution can be used to find the answer to a certain class of probability problem – those where each event has two possible outcomes.

It is important to note that only the basic principles of probability introduced in Chapter 4 have been used in the construction of the binomial. Despite the use of a number of equations, no new conceptual ideas have been introduced here. Rather, what has been done is to develop methods to evaluate these ideas in practice and to indicate some ways in which they might be applied to business problems. The next chapter takes this process further.

Reference

The following article considers the problem of overbooking further. Although the article is not situated specifically in a probability context, notice how many empirical probabilities are given:

TOH, R. (1986), 'Coping with no-shows, late cancellations and oversales: American hotels out-do the airlines', *International Journal of Hospitality Management*, **5(3)**: 121–125.

Exercises

1 Over a long period of time, it is observed that the average carry over for a hotel is 35%. Of ten guests registered for a particular night find the probability that:

(a) none stays the following night;
(b) one stays
(c) two stay
(d) three stay
(e) four stay
(f) five stay.

Present your results as a probability histogram.

2 A hotel receives telephone bookings that are too late to be confirmed in writing. It knows from experience that on average 95% of such bookings are fulfilled. If on a particular night 5 unconfirmed telephone bookings have been received, find the probability that:

(a) all bookings are honoured;
(b) at least one is dishonoured;
(c) exactly one is dishonoured;
(d) more than two are dishonoured.

3 On average, 50% of guests take dinner in the hotel restaurant on the night they arrive at the hotel. If on a particular night 30 guests are registered, how many meals would you recommend be prepared and why?

4 A hotel chain uses the number of complaints received from its customers as a simple indicator of the standard of service being achieved by its hotels. However, management knows that even if the service is at a level considered to be satisfactory, some guests will complain about something. The last time a survey was conducted, it was found that about a 5% unjustified complaint level was to be expected.

The chain now wishes to check that 5% remains the correct figure. To this end, it has taken 1,000 random samples, each sample being of 5 guests, from its hotels around the country. If the 5% figure is correct, in how many of the samples would you expect to find:

(a) less than two complaints;
(b) more than three complaints?

Appendix
Listing of BASIC program to calculate binomial probabilities

```
10 KEY OFF:CLS
20 LOCATE 1,10:PRINT "Programme to calculate binomial probabilities"
30 LOCATE 3,10:PRINT "Enter initial value for n        ":LOCATE 3,37:INPUT N
40 IF N>0 THEN 60
50 LOCATE 5,10:PRINT "Error - n must exceed zero":GOTO 30
60 LOCATE 5,10:PRINT "Enter initial value for p        ":LOCATE 5,37:INPUT P
70 IF P>0 AND P<1 THEN 170
80 LOCATE 7,10:PRINT "Error - p must be between 0 and 1":GOTO 60
89 REM
90 REM *** Sub routine to calculate probability ***
91 REM *** ================================== ***
92 REM
100 P5=P^X*((1-P)^(N-X))
110 D=N-X
120 IF D>X THEN N1=X ELSE N1=D
130 FOR J1=0 TO N1-1
140     P5=P5*((N-J1)/(N1-J1))
150 NEXT J1
160 RETURN
169 REM
170 REM *** Main menu ***
171 REM *** ========= ***
172 REM
180 CLS
190 LOCATE 1,10:PRINT "Programme to calculate binomial probabilities"
200 LOCATE 3,10:PRINT "Current value of n is ";N
210 LOCATE 5,10:PRINT "Current value of p is ";P
220 LOCATE 8,10:PRINT "A  -  Change values of n and/or p"
230 LOCATE 10,10:PRINT "B  -  Probability that X equals a particular value"
240 LOCATE 12,10:PRINT "C  -  Probability that X is greater than a particular
value"
250 LOCATE 20,10:PRINT "X  -  Exit program"
260 A$=INKEY$:IF A$<>"A" AND A$<>"a" AND  A$<>"B" AND  A$<>"b" AND  A$<>"C" AND
A$<>"c" AND A$<>"X" AND A$<>"x" THEN 260
270 IF A$="A" OR A$="a" THEN 320
280 IF A$="B" OR A$="b" THEN 400
290 IF A$="C" OR A$="c" THEN 510
300 IF A$="X" OR A$="x" THEN CLS:END
309 REM
310 REM *** Procedure to change current values of n and/or p ***
```

```
311 REM *** ================================================= ***
312 REM
320 CLS
330 LOCATE 1,10:PRINT "Procedure to change current values of n and/or p"
340 LOCATE  8,10:PRINT "Current value of n is ";N:LOCATE 10,10:PRINT "Enter new
value or hit return to keep this value ";:INPUT NN$
350 IF VAL(NN$)>0 THEN N=VAL(NN$):GOTO 370 ELSE IF VAL(NN$)=0 THEN 370
360 LOCATE 14,10:PRINT "Error - n must exceed zero":GOTO 340
370 LOCATE 14,10:PRINT "Current value of p is ";P:LOCATE 16,10:PRINT "Enter new
value or hit return to keep this value ";:INPUT NP$
380 IF  VAL(NP$)>0 AND  VAL(NP$)<1 THEN  P=VAL(NP$):GOTO 170 ELSE IF VAL(NP$)=0
THEN 170
390 LOCATE 18,10:PRINT "Error - p must be between 0 and 1":GOTO 370
399 REM
400 REM *** Procedure to calculate probability X equals some value ***
401 REM *** ================================================= ***
402 REM
410 CLS
420 LOCATE 1,10:PRINT "Procedure to calculate probability X equals a particular
value"
430 LOCATE 10,10:PRINT "Enter value of X            ":LOCATE 10,29:INPUT X
440 IF X>=0 AND X<=N THEN 460
450 LOCATE  15,10:PRINT "Error  - X  cannot be negative or greater than n":GOTO
430
460 GOSUB 90
470 LOCATE  15,10:PRINT "Given  n=";N;" and  p=";P;" probability  of X=";X;" is
";:PRINT USING "£.££££££££";P5
480 LOCATE  23,9:COLOR 0,7:PRINT  " Hit the space bar to return to menu ":COLOR
7,0
490 A$=INKEY$:IF A$<>" " THEN 490
500 GOTO 170
509 REM
510 REM *** Procedure to calculate probability X greater than value ***
511 REM *** ================================================= ***
512 REM
520 CLS
530 LOCATE 1,10:PRINT "Procedure to  calculate  probability  X  greater  than a
particular value"
540 LOCATE 10,10:PRINT "Enter value of X            ":LOCATE 10,29:INPUT XX
550 IF XX>=0 AND XX<=N THEN 570
560 LOCATE  15,10:PRINT "Error  - X  cannot be negative or greater than n":GOTO
540
570 P6=0:LOCATE 18,10:PRINT "Computing ... please wait"
580 FOR X=XX+1 TO N
590     GOSUB 90
600     P6=P6+P5
610 NEXT
620 LOCATE 18,10:PRINT SPC(25)
630 LOCATE 15,10:PRINT "Given  n=";N;" and  p=";P;" probability  of X>";XX;" is
";:PRINT USING "£.££££££££";P6
640 LOCATE  15,9:COLOR 0,7:PRINT  " Hit the space bar to return to menu ":COLOR
7,0
650 A$=INKEY$:IF A$<>" " THEN 650
660 P6=0:GOTO 170
```

7
The normal probability distribution

The previous chapter discussed the binomial probability distribution, which is perhaps the most important of those distributions relating to discrete data – i.e. where the data set may only take on particular values: stay/don't stay, yes/no and so on. The normal distribution is the most important of the continuous distributions – i.e. those related to variables that may take on any value. As we shall see below, many phenomena, which are actually discrete and should be described by a distribution such as the binomial, may be approximated by the normal distribution. The use of the normal greatly simplifies probability calculations. Before we can go on to discuss the use of the normal to approximate other distributions, we need first to consider the normal distribution itself.

The equation of the normal curve

Chapters 2 and 3 concerning data classification and summary showed that a data set which has a symmetrical distribution is centred on its arithmetic mean, and spreads around the mean according to its standard deviation. This is the case with the normal distribution. Once we know the mean and standard deviation of a normal distribution then it is possible to draw it, although to be able to do so requires knowledge of the equation of the normal curve. The credit for establishing the normal distribution is usually given to the 19th century German mathematician Karl-Friedrich Gauss (1777–1855), although Gauss himself acknowledged the French mathematician Laplace (1749–1827) as its originator. In any event, the normal is sometimes also called the Gaussian curve, and its equation is as follows:

$$y = \frac{1}{\sigma \times \sqrt{(2\pi)}} \times e^{-z/2} \text{ where } z = [\,(x - \mu)/\sigma\,]^2 \qquad (7.1)$$

As is apparent the development of Equation (7.1) represented a phenomenal feat. Fortunately, if we now wish to see what the normal curve looks like, all that is required is to program a computer to plot out the values of y calculated by Equation (7.1) for different values of x.

Notice that we only need to know two things to be able to draw the curve – the mean and the standard deviation. Once we know these two values then we can draw the normal curve precisely. Notice also that we will get a different normal curve for each set of mean and standard deviation values that we use. It is traditional to describe normal curves and distributions in terms of their mean and variance, using the following notation:

$$X \sim N(\mu, \sigma^2)$$

This is interpreted to mean that X is a normally-distributed random variable having mean, μ, and *variance*, σ^2. We might have for instance:

$$X \sim N(25, 25)$$

which would then be interpreted to mean that X is a random variable having a normal distribution with arithmetic mean 25 and variance 25 (and hence standard deviation 5). Notice that once more the notation is used merely as a shorthand, however complicated it may appear at first sight.

The normal curve and probability

Although the fundamental shape of the curve will remain the same, its location and spread will depend, of course, on the values assigned to the mean and standard deviation. Figure 7.1 shows three normal curves drawn for different values.

So far we have become accustomed to the idea of the normal curve as a frequency curve summarizing the histogram. How then may this curve be used in the calculation of probabilities? The answer is as follows. The total area beneath the curve represents all possible outcomes. This area may be standardized to a value of one, regardless of its true value. This procedure is acceptable because with probability we are interested, as we saw in Chapter 4, in the fraction: favourable outcomes/total outcomes. We then identify the area beneath the curve that corresponds to favourable outcomes and express this as a fraction of the total area. The result is the probability figure in which we are interested.

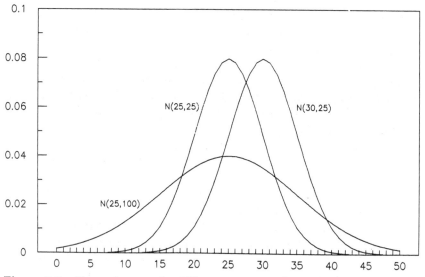

Figure 7.1   *Normal curves for different means and standard deviations*

Suppose, for example, that the time that a customer (or set of customers) occupies a table in a restaurant is normally distributed with mean 100 minutes and variance 400 (i.e. $N(100, 400)$). What is the probability that a table will remain occupied for more than 100 minutes? We know that the distribution is symmetrical about its mean which is here 100. Hence half of the curve must lie to the right of 100 and half to the left. The area to the right corresponds to favourable outcomes in this problem and the probability of a table remaining occupied for more than 100 minutes is therefore 0.5. We do not need to know the true areas beneath the curve to find this answer; as we have just seen, we merely need to know the proportion of the area corresponding to favourable outcomes.

It may occur to some readers that there is a problem with this answer. If the probability of $X>100$ is 0.5, then by the same logic the probability of $X<100$ must also be 0.5. However, this would imply that the probability that $X=100$ is zero, but this must be incorrect since $X=100$ is the arithmetic mean and therefore the most likely single outcome! The problem is more apparent than real, however, and is explained by the fact that the normal distribution is continuous. In such cases, it does not make sense to attempt to calculate the probability of particular values, such as 100. In the example above, the variable is time. The mean is given in terms of minutes but the measurement of time may be as accurate as we wish, subject only to the accuracy of the measuring instrument. Hence more than 100 minutes could be interpreted as 100.000 000 000 000 0001 (or as many zeros before the 1 as you wish) minutes or more; and less than 100 minutes as 99.999 999 999 999 999 (etc.) and less. Once we define values as accurately as this, it is clear that the chances of anybody staying precisely 100 minutes are indeed zero.

Rather than trying to calculate the probabilities of precise values, the normal distribution must be used to calculate the probability that X lies between particular values, for instance we can find the probability that the time a table remains occupied is between 99.5 and 100.5 minutes. In this case we would have arbitrarily divided the continuous variable time into discrete lumps – minutes. Depending on the purpose of the probability calculations this division may or may not be sufficiently accurate. If we wish to be more accurate we would work in half-minute units. In this case we would approximate the probability that the time spent was 100 minutes by the probability that it was between 99.75 and 100.25. In certain problems (e.g. quality control), a high level of accuracy may be necessary but this is not generally the case in business-related situations. In the problem above, the probability that a table remains occupied for 100 minutes could be approximated, for example, by the range 80–120 minutes for practical purposes.

The calculation of probability using the normal distribution may be achieved in a number of ways. First (and most difficult), we could proceed from first principles and calculate the area beneath the curve between the values of X that are of interest. This would require that we use calculus to integrate the equation of the curve between the chosen limits. Second, as with the binomial, it is not too difficult to program a computer to undertake the calculations and a BASIC program that does this is presented in the appendix to this chapter. Third, (and most commonly), we can use probability tables which exist based upon the normal distribution. To use these, we first use the coding method introduced in Chapter 3 to standardize the normal distribution. As we saw in Chapter 3, with coding the trick is to standardize as simply as possible. The simplest normal distribution is that having a mean of zero and a variance of one ($N(0,1)$) and this is therefore the one that has been chosen by statisticians as the basis for standardization. It is consequently known as the *standard normal distribution*. Using the coding method *any* normal distribution may be standardized. Tables of probabilities are widely available for the standard normal distribution. The ones referred to here are again those of Murdoch and Barnes.

The standard normal distribution

Let us look first of all at how we standardize the normal distribution. We know that the time spent at each table is distributed as N(100, 400). The normal curve is centred on 100 and spreads around this value according to the standard deviation of 20 minutes (remember it is the *variance* that is 400). This curve is sketched in Figure 7.2. It runs from a value of 40 minutes (which is the mean less 3 standard deviations) to 160 minutes (which is the mean plus 3 standard deviations). To find the probability, for example, that a table will be occupied between 80 and 120 minutes, we need to find the shaded area as a proportion of the total.

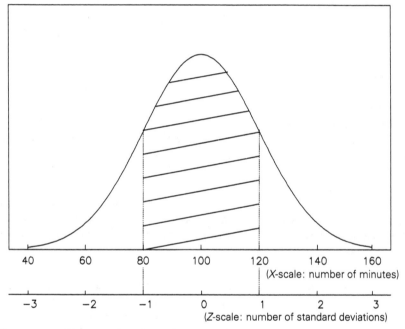

Figure 7.2   *Change of scale with standard normal distribution*

The standardization of the scale is carried out using the coding method as before. Remember that we have the basic formula

$$u = \frac{x - a}{b}$$

In this case, we let *a* equal the arithmetic mean and *b* equal the standard deviation. The standardized distribution is then centred on zero and spreads around the mean following the simple progression $-3, -2, -1, 0, 1, 2, 3$ – that is, it is distributed normally with mean zero and variance (and standard deviation) one: $N(0, 1)$. Table 7.1 presents the standardization of the table occupancy times.

Table 7.1 *The standardization of a normal distribution*

General form	Example value	Standardized value
Mean $-$ 3s.d.	40	$(40 - 100)/20 = -3$
Mean $-$ 2s.d.	60	$(60 - 100)/20 = -2$
Mean $-$ 1s.d.	80	$(80 - 100)/20 = -1$
Mean $-$ 0s.d.	100	$(100 - 100)/20 = 0$
Mean $+$ 1s.d.	120	$(120 - 100)/20 = 1$
Mean $+$ 2s.d.	140	$(140 - 100)/20 = 2$
Mean $+$ 3s.d.	160	$(160 - 100)/20 = 3$

Regardless of the distribution we have to begin with, it may be standardized to the form shown in Table 7.1. The standardized values are usually called the Z-values. As shown by Figure 7.2, if we wish to find the probability that X lies between 80 and 120 when we have an $N(100, 400)$ then this is equivalent to finding the probability that Z lies between -1 i.e. $(80 - 100)/20$ and $+1$ $(120 - 100)/20$ when we have an $N(0, 1)$. These latter two probabilities may be found directly from the tables which exist for the standard normal distribution. Let us look at the use of these tables.

The use of standard normal probability tables

A number of kinds of probability table exist but their use is similar. The tables discussed here are those which seem to be most commonly used. They are presented in Murdoch and Barnes as Table 3 (page 13). The first thing that is apparent is that the tables only give probabilities for positive values of Z; the reason being that, as the normal distribution is symmetrical, the probabilities for the corresponding negative values may be found from the positive ones. The tables give the area to the right of different Z-values.

Rule 1 The probability that Z will exceed any non-negative value is read directly from the table. For instance, $P(Z>1)$, shown in Figure 7.3(a), is found immediately as 0.1587.

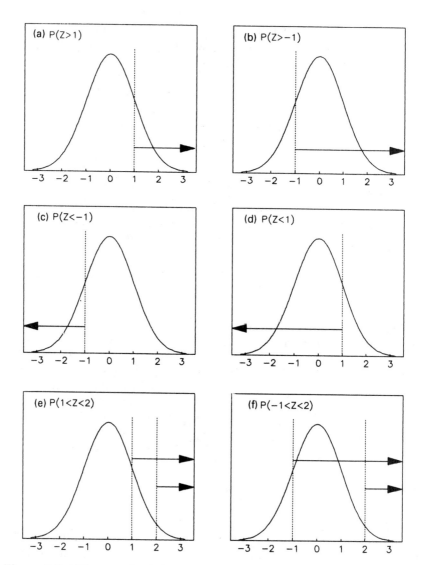

Figure 7.3   *The use of standard normal probability tables*

Rule 2   The probability that Z exceeds a negative value requires that use is made of the facts that the area beneath the curve is one and that the normal distribution is symmetrical. For example, what is P(Z> −1)? As is clear from Figure 7.3(b), this probability is equal to the whole area beneath the curve (which is one) minus the area to the left of the Z-value, that is,

$$P(Z> -1) = 1 - P(Z< -1).$$

Since the normal distribution is symmetrical, the area to the left of -1 must be the same as the area to the right of $+1$, that is,

$$P(Z<-1) = P(Z>1).$$

As we have just seen, this latter probability may be read directly from the tables. Thus the probability that Z exceeds -1 is found as:

$$P(Z> -1) = 1 - P(Z< -1) = 1 - P(Z>1) = 1 - 0.1587 = 0.8413$$

Rule 3   To find the probability of Z being less than a given value, we reverse the logic above. The probability of Z less than any negative value is straightforward. For example, $P(Z<-1)$, Figure 7.3(c), is the same as $P(Z>1)$ and this latter may be read from the tables.

Rule 4   The probability of Z being less than a positive value, such as one, is found (Figure 7.3(d)) as:

$$P(Z<1) = 1 - P(Z>1) = 0.8413$$

Rule 5   To find the probability of Z being between two values, we break the problem into its component parts. The use of a sketch along the lines of Figure 7.3(e) is strongly recommended. We then apply one of the above rules to the calculation of each of the two probabilities and subtract the smaller value from the larger one. For instance, suppose we wish to find the probability that Z lies between 1 and 2. If we find the probability that Z exceeds one and then subtract the probability that Z exceeds two then we shall be left with the area that we require, i.e.

$$P(1<Z<2) = P(Z>1) - P(Z>2) = 0.1587 - 0.02275 = 0.13595$$

Rule 6   Suppose now that we wished to find the probability that Z lies between -1 and -2 (not drawn). We have:

$$P(-2<Z<-1)$$

which because of the symmetrical nature of the normal is precisely the same as

$$P(1<Z<2) = 0.13595 \text{ (from above).}$$

Rule 7   The final kind of problem that must be considered is where the area of interest straddles the mean. For instance suppose that we wish to find the probability that Z lies between −1 and +2 (Figure 7.3(f)),

$$P(-1<Z<2) = P(Z>-1) - P(Z>2)$$

but from rule 2 above $P(Z>-1) = 1 - P(Z>1)$
Hence

$$P(-1<Z<2) = 1 - P(Z>1) - P(Z>2) = 1 - 0.1587 - 0.02275 = 0.81855$$

Table 7.2   *Summary of rules for use of normal probability tables*

1. $P(Z>a)$ read directly from tables
2. $P(Z>-a) = 1 - P(Z>a)$
3. $P(Z<-a) = P(Z>a)$
4. $P(Z<a) = 1 - P(Z>a)$
5. $P(a<Z<b) = P(Z>a) - P(Z>b)$
6. $P(-b<Z<-a) = P(Z>a) - P(Z>b)$
7. $P(-b>Z>a) = 1 - P(Z>b) - P(Z>a)$

The normal approximation to the binomial

As the example above concerning occupancy times for tables in a restaurant makes clear, the normal distribution may be used directly to calculate probabilities in the case of continuous variables. It also has an important role to play in the calculation of probabilities in the case of discrete (e.g. binomial) variables. In such cases the probability histogram may often be approximated by a normal curve and the standard normal probability tables may then be used, greatly facilitating probability calculations. In this section, we will look at this use of the normal with respect to the binomial.

We saw, in one of the exercises following Chapter 6, that binomial probabilities may be depicted graphically in the form of a probability histogram. Thus rather than finding the probability of an event via the binomial formula, we could instead find the area of the appropriate bar in the histogram. If this histogram is approximated by a normal curve then instead of finding the area of the bar, we may find the area beneath the normal curve corresponding to that bar.

However, we seem to face a difficulty at this point. Since there is an infinite number of normal curves, which one should be used? The answer is that we use the one that best 'fits' the histogram. If asked to draw a normal curve onto a binomial probability histogram freehand, most people find it natural that the peak of the curve should correspond

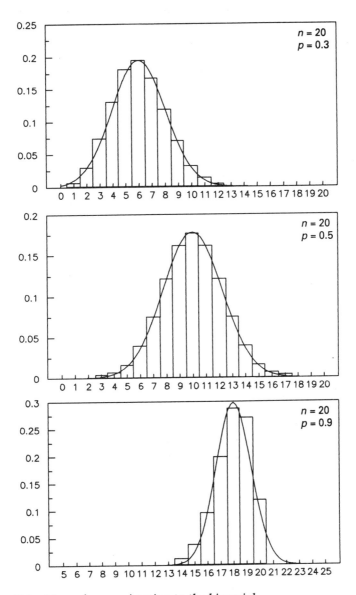

Figure 7.4   *Normal approximation to the binomial*

to the peak of the binomial and that the spread of the normal should be similar to that of the binomial. This intuitive solution is in fact correct. The normal curve providing the best approximation to a binomial histogram will be the one that has the same mean (peak) and variance (spread) as the histogram. The mean of a binomial is given as: $n \times p$; and the variance is: $n \times p \times q$.

Figure 7.4 presents three binomial histograms with their appropriate normal approximations. In each case the number of trials (n) is 20. As might be expected, the approximation is better in the case where the binomial is symmetrical ($p=0.5$). As the distribution becomes skewed, so the approximation becomes increasingly poor. In the case where $p=0.3$ (a slight positive skew) the approximation remains reasonably good, although it is clear that an error is introduced by using the normal curve rather than the binomial. In the case where $p=0.9$ (a quite large negative skew) the error is relatively large. Table 7.3 gives the probabilities calculated using the binomial formula and the normal approximation for this case. As may be seen, the error is greatest in the case where $X=19$. Whether this error is of any *practical* significance depends on the case under consideration. In situations where the error does matter, it is obvious that the normal approximation cannot be used. Note, however, that the approximation becomes increasingly good as n increases regardless of the value of p.

Table 7.4 shows the difference between probabilities calculated using the binomial formula and the normal approximation. The probability of success on a single trial is held constant at 0.9 and the value of n is varied. To provide a comparison, the probability of obtaining precisely the mean value is calculated for each n. It is apparent from the table that the relative error decreases systematically as n increases. A reasonable approximation (error less than 1%) is reached quite fast despite the skew in the binomial histogram. The results presented in Table 7.4 support the frequently-used *decision rule* that:

the normal approximation to the binomial should be used only in those cases where both $n \times p$ and $n \times q$ are greater than 5.

Table 7.3   *The normal approximation to the binomial with a skewed distribution. The difference between binomial and normal probabilities when $p=0.9$.*

x	Binomial probability	Normal probability
14	0.00887	0.00415
15	0.03192	0.02666
16	0.08978	0.10057
17	0.19012	0.22292
18	0.28518	0.29067
19	0.27017	0.22292
20	0.12158	0.13175

In the example presented in Table 7.4 this would mean that only in cases where n exceeded 50 would the approximation be used. As we can see the use of this rule would ensure accurate results.

However, while the above decision rule is *sufficient* to ensure accurate results, it may not be *necessary*. Where the binomial distribution is symmetrical, good results are obtained even with very small n values. The following example illustrates this point while serving as a guide as to how precisely to apply the normal distribution to the binomial.

Consider again the example introduced in the previous chapter of a machine which accepts or rejects items according to their weight. Suppose, however, that at present, 50% of items are accepted. What is the probability that the next three items on the production line are accepted?

As we know, this is a trivial binomial problem. Its solution is straightforward and in practice there would be no point in using the normal approximation. In fact, in practice even the binomial would not be used since the solution to the problem is readily obtained from first principles (multiplication theorem of probability). However, the problem is useful here to demonstrate how the normal approximation is applied and to check that the results are reasonable. We have then $n=3$ and $p=0.5$.

The set of possible results is presented in Table 7.5.

In this example, the mean value is: $n \times p = 3 \times 0.5 = 1.5$ and the variance is: $n \times p \times q = 3 \times 0.5 \times 0.5 = 0.75$. Hence the binomial probability histogram may be approximated by the normal curve $N(1.5, 0.75)$. The histogram and curve are shown in Figure 7.5.

Table 7.4 *The difference between binomial and normal probabilities as n increases (p=0.9)*

n	X	Binomial probability	Normal probability	Relative error (per cent)
10	9	0.38742	0.40190	3.74
20	18	0.28518	0.29067	1.93
40	36	0.20589	0.20791	0.98
60	54	0.16929	0.17043	0.67
80	72	0.14712	0.14788	0.52
100	90	0.13187	0.13243	0.42
120	108	0.12055	0.12099	0.36
140	126	0.11172	0.11208	0.32
160	144	0.10458	0.10489	0.30
180	162	0.09866	0.09893	0.27
200	180	0.09364	0.09388	0.26

Table 7.5   *Possible outcomes and their probabilities: quality control*

Event	Favourable outcomes	Probability
3 accepts	AAA	1/8
2 accepts	AAR ARA RAA	3/8
1 accept	ARR RAR AAR	3/8
0 accepts	RRR	1/8
	8 possible outcomes	

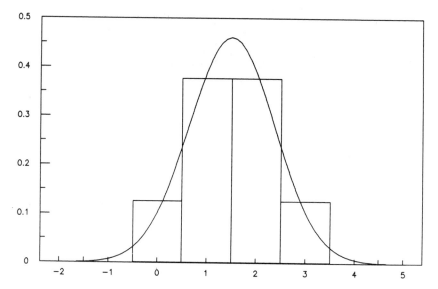

Figure 7.5   *Normal approximation to the binomial with small symmetrical sample*

How then do we use the normal curve to find the probabilities? Before looking at the problem of finding the probability of three accepts, which is one of the two extreme outcomes, let us consider the two central values, beginning with the probability of obtaining exactly one accept, i.e. $P(X=1)$. We already know that this is equal to 3/8. Let us see how we can find approximately the same answer using the normal distribution rather than the binomial.

Looking at the binomial histogram, we can see that the value $X=1$ corresponds to the bar going from 0.5 to 1.5. Hence we must find the area beneath the normal curve between these limits. The problem of finding the probability of obtaining one accept may be written either in binomial form or in normal form, that is

$$P(X=1) \quad = \quad P(0.5 < X < 1.5)$$
$$\text{Binomial} \qquad\qquad \text{Normal}$$

The difference between the two arises from the fact that we are using a continuous distribution to approximate a discrete one. This kind of correction must always be made when using the normal approximation to the binomial. The *general rule* is:

$$P(X=a) \quad = \quad P(a-0.5 < X < a+0.5)$$
$$\text{Binomial} \qquad\qquad \text{Normal}$$

Having got this far, the probability is found by standardizing the normal in the usual way – i.e. we subtract the mean (1.5) and divide by the standard deviation (0.87), giving

$$P\left(\frac{0.5 - 1.5}{0.87} < Z < \frac{1.5 - 1.5}{0.87} \right) = P(-1.15 < Z < 0)$$

From *rule 6* for the use of the standard normal tables, this probability is found to be 0.3749 (i.e. almost exactly 3/8).

The procedure for finding the probability of obtaining two accepts is the same. We begin by defining the problem in terms of the binomial and then translate it to the normal distribution. We then standardize and find the answer from the normal tables. This procedure gives:

$$P(X=2) \quad = \quad P(1.5 < X < 2.5) \quad = \quad P(0 < Z < 1.15)$$
$$\text{Binomial} \qquad\quad \text{Normal} \qquad\qquad \text{Standard Normal}$$

The probability of $X=2$ is the mirror image of the probability of $X=1$ and the answer is again 0.3749.

In all problems where the normal distribution is used to approximate the binomial, to find the probability that X is equal to a particular value the adjustment of 0.5 either side of the value must be made. The only exception concerns the case of end values. Consider, for instance, the probability of obtaining no accepts. If we use the same technique as previously then we would write the problem as follows:

$$P(X=0) = P(-0.5 < X < 0.5)$$

This however is incorrect because, as is clear from **Figure 7.5**, the normal distribution continues beyond the value -0.5. Since there is no possibility of obtaining -1 accepts, the area beyond -0.5 will be left unassigned if we proceed as above. The best approximation requires that this area be assigned to the end value. We therefore ignore the lower limit on the normal version of the problem so that it is re-written as:

$$P(X=0) = P(X < 0.5)$$

Standardizing and using the tables we obtain 0.1144 as the result for the first version and a value of 0.1251 for the second. Since we know that the true value is 1/8 (=0.125) it is obvious that the latter version of the problem is the correct one to use.

Finally to find the probability of getting three accepts, we have by similar reasoning:

$$P(X=3) = P(X > 2.5)$$

which is again equal to 0.1251.

The *general rule* introduced above must therefore be slightly modified:

$P(X=a) = P(a-0.5 < X < a+0.5)$ except
$P(X=a) = P(X < a+0.5)$ where X is the low end-value and
$P(X=a) = P(X > a-0.5)$ where X is the high end-value.

The above example demonstrates (a) how to use the normal distribution to calculate binomial probabilities and (b) that in most cases the results will be sufficiently accurate for decision-making purposes. It should be clear that while the fundamental theorems of probability may always be used to solve problems, on many occasions it will be easier and just as accurate to use the binomial or normal instead. One purpose of the examples has been to show that this use is legitimate. Let us now turn to some applications where the binomial and normal are more obviously useful.

Normal approximation to the binomial: an application

Suppose that a hotel has 30 guests staying a particular night. From past records the hotel manager knows that the probability that any one guest asks to remain the following night is 0.4. What is the probability that exactly 10 guests ask to stay on?

This is clearly a binomial problem since it meets the conditions that we set out previously (see Chapter 6) – in particular each 'trial' (i.e. guest) has only two possible outcomes: either they stay on or they do not. We may tackle this problem either by using the binomial distribution directly or by using the normal approximation to it. As a final check on accuracy and also on technique let us solve the problem in both ways.

The basic parameters of the problem are: $n=30$, $p=0.4$ (defining success as that guests stay on), $q=0.6$. The probability that exactly 10 people stay on is then given as:

$$P(X=10) \;=\; \underset{10}{\overset{30}{C}} \quad \overset{10}{0.4} \;\bullet\; \overset{20}{0.6} \;=\; 0.1151854$$

Unfortunately, most binomial tables do not include values for $n=30$. However, if you have entered into the computer the program presented in the Appendix to Chapter 6, you can find the solution using that. Alternatively, the solution is fairly readily found with a pocket calculator.

Using the normal approximation we have:

$$\underset{\text{Binomial}}{P(X=10)} \quad = \quad \underset{\text{Normal}}{P(9.5 < X < 10.5)}$$

The mean is: $np = 30 \times 0.4 = 12$ and the variance: $npq = 30 \times 0.4 \times 0.6 = 7.2$ (implying a standard deviation of 2.68).
Standardizing gives:

$$P\left(\frac{9.5 - 12}{2.68} < Z < \frac{10.5 - 12}{2.68} \right)$$

$$= P\left(-0.93 < Z < -0.56 \right)$$

which applying *rule 6* of Table 7.2 concerning the use of standard normal probability tables is found to equal 0.1115. In other words, the error involved is very small and is almost certainly acceptable at least for business applications of probability.

At the moment the advantage of using the normal approximation rather than the binomial formula is not clear. Consider, however, the following problem. Suppose that instead of finding the probability of *exactly* ten people staying on you are asked to find the probability that *at least* ten stay on. If you now wish to use the binomial you will have to consider the following probabilities.

$$P(X>=10) = P(X=10) + P(X=11) + P(X=12) + \dots + P(X=30)$$

This can in fact be made slightly less tedious by calculating

$$1 - \{ P(X=0) + P(X=1) + \dots + P(X=9) \}$$

Compare however the normal approach to the same problem:

$$P(X>=10) = P(X>9.5) = P(Z>-0.934) = 0.8238$$
$$\text{Binomial} \quad \text{Normal} \quad \text{Standard Normal}$$

using *rule* 2 of Table 7.2.

If you work through the binomial version of the problem above you should obtain the result that the probability is 0.82371352. As can be seen the error resulting from the use of the normal is once again minimal and here the time saved is considerable.

Notice finally that in the transformation from binomial to normal in the above problem, 0.5 has been subtracted from the X-value. This is because the binomial version reads X greater than *or equal to* 10 – hence 10 must be included, which gives greater than 9.5 in the normal version. Were the problem to be changed so that the binomial version read X greater than 10, then 0.5 would be added to the normal version to ensure that the value 10 were excluded from the calculations. When moving from binomial to normal versions of a problem always ask yourself whether limiting values should be excluded or included and make the 0.5 adjustments accordingly.

Conclusion

In this chapter we have seen how the probability of events having a normal distribution may be calculated. The standardization of distributions has been demonstrated as has the use of the standard normal probability tables. The listing of a BASIC program which calculates normal probabilities is presented in the appendix to the chapter.

The normal distribution is important first because many phenomena are naturally normally distributed but even more so because many phenomena may be approximated by a normal distribution provided that the sample size is large enough. For this reason the normal distribution plays a central role in statistics. This chapter has considered one case where the normal is used to approximate another distribution – that of the normal approximation to the binomial. This case is probably the most important from a business viewpoint.

The next chapter takes the application of probability distributions much further when we begin to look at the use of such distributions to test statistical hypotheses and to aid decision-making in uncertain situations.

Exercises

1   Suppose that X is a normally distributed random variable with mean, μ, and variance, σ^2 – i.e. $N(\mu, \sigma^2)$. Use the standard normal distribution to find:
   (a) $P(X<15)$ when $\mu=10$ and $\sigma^2=16$;
   (b) $P(X>0)$ when $\mu=1$ and $\sigma=1$;
   (c) $P(11<X<15)$ when $\mu=12$ and $\sigma^2=25$.

2   Continuing Exercise 4 from Chapter 6, if each sample size is increased to 80, use the normal approximation to the binomial to find the number of samples containing:
   (a) between 8 and 12 complaints;
   (b) less than 4 complaints.

3   Continuing Exercise 3 from Chapter 6. In the case of telephone reservations received more than a month in advance the probability that they will be fulfilled drops to 80%. If the hotel has 100 such bookings, find the probability that:
   (a) 75 arrive;
   (b) 82 arrive.
      The hotel decides that it will only allocate sufficient rooms to such reservations that there is a 5% chance of being left with one or more empty rooms. How many rooms (to the nearest integer) should therefore be allocated to the 100 guests?
      How many rooms should be allocated if the hotel decides that it only wants a 1% chance of being left with empty rooms?

4   Experience suggests that new restaurant businesses have a 25% chance of failing within their first 5 years. Out of 100 such businesses created during a year, find the probability that:
   (a) all are still in business after 5 years;
   (b) exactly 25 fail during the first 5-year period;
   (c) between 18 and 30 fail during the first 5-year period.

Appendix
Basic listing of program to calculate probabilities using normal distribution

```
10 KEY OFF:CLS:GOTO 370: REM *** Enter basic parameters ***
20 REM
30 REM *** Sub routine for probability calculations ***
40 REM     ========================================
50 REM
60 PZ=0:PROB1 = .3989422*(EXP(-(Z^2)/2))
70 FOR ZZ=Z+PAS TO 4 STEP PAS
80     PROB2 = .3989422*(EXP(-(ZZ^2)/2))
90     PROB = ((PROB1+PROB2)/2)*PAS
100    PROB1=PROB2
110    PZ = PZ+PROB
120 NEXT ZZ
130 RETURN
140 REM
150 REM *** Main menu ***
160 REM     =========
170 REM
180 CLS:PRINT "Programme to calculate probabilities using normal distribution"
190 LOCATE 3,10:PRINT "Basic data presently as follows"
200 LOCATE 5,10:PRINT "Mean ...................... ";M
210 LOCATE 6,10:PRINT "Standard deviation ........ ";S
220 LOCATE 7,10:PRINT "Accuracy (decimal places) .. ";(LOG(ACC)/LOG(10))-1
230 LOCATE 8,10:PRINT "No of steps in calculation . ";1/PAS
240 LOCATE 10,10:PRINT "A  -  Change basic parameters"
250 LOCATE 12,10:PRINT "B  -  Calculate probability that X greater than a given
value"
260 LOCATE 14,10:PRINT "C  -  Calculate probability that X less than a given
value"
270 LOCATE 16,10:PRINT "D  -  Calculate probability that X lies between two
values"
280 LOCATE 20,10:PRINT "X  -  Exit programme"
290 LOCATE 24,10:PRINT "Choose an option";
300 OPT$=INKEY$:IF OPT$<>"A" AND OPT$<>"a" AND OPT$<>"B" AND OPT$<>"b" AND
OPT$<>"C" AND OPT$<>"c" AND OPT$<>"D" AND OPT$<>"d" AND OPT$<>"X" AND OPT$<>"x"
THEN 300
310 IF OPT$="A" OR OPT$="a" THEN 370
320 IF OPT$="B" OR OPT$="b" THEN 570
330 IF OPT$="C" OR OPT$="c" THEN 760
340 IF OPT$="D" OR OPT$="d" THEN 940
350 CLS:END
```

```
360 REM
370 REM *** Procedure to enter/change basic parameters ***
380 REM    ==========================================
390 REM
400 CLS
410 PRINT "Procedure to enter/change basic parameters"
420 LOCATE 4,1:PRINT "Enter basic data"
430 LOCATE 8,1:INPUT "Mean ................ ";M
440 LOCATE 10,1:INPUT "Standard deviation ... ";S
450 IF S<>0 THEN 470
460 LOCATE 12,1:PRINT "Error - Standard deviation cannot be zero":GOTO 440
470 LOCATE 12,1:PRINT "Accuracy of calculations (number of places after decimal
point)
480 LOCATE 13,1:INPUT "Choose 3, 4, 5 or 6 places";ACC
490 IF ACC<>3 AND ACC<>4 AND ACC<>5 AND ACC<>6 THEN 480
500 IF ACC=3 THEN ACC$="#.###" ELSE IF ACC=4 THEN ACC$="#.####" ELSE IF ACC=5
THEN ACC$="#.#####" ELSE ACC$="#.######"
510 ACC=10^(ACC+1)
520 LOCATE 15,1:PRINT "Enter number of steps in probability calculation"
530 LOCATE 17,1:PRINT "Note: a value of 100 is generally sufficiently accurate.
Less steps than this"
540 LOCATE 18,1:PRINT "results in errors. The more steps you have, the longer
the calculations take."
550 LOCATE 20,1:INPUT "Number of steps ";PAS
560 IF PAS>0 THEN PAS=1/PAS:GOTO 150 ELSE GOTO 550: REM *** Return to menu ***
570 REM
580 REM *** Procedure to calculate prob that X greater than some number ***
590 REM    =========================================================
600 REM
610 CLS
620 PRINT "Procedure to calculate probability that X greater than a given
value"
630 LOCATE 5,10:INPUT "Enter value of X";X
640 Z=(X-M)/S
650 IF Z=0 THEN RESULT=.5:GOTO 690
660 IF Z<0 THEN Z=Z*-1:H=1 ELSE H=0
670 GOSUB 60
680 IF H=0 THEN RESULT=PZ ELSE IF H=1 THEN RESULT=1-PZ
690 LOCATE 18,10:PRINT "Given a mean of ";M;" and a standard deviation of ";S
700 LOCATE 20,10:PRINT "the probability of X greater than ";X
710 LOCATE 22,10:PRINT "is ";:PRINT USING ACC$;(INT(RESULT*ACC)/ACC)
720 LOCATE 24,25:COLOR 0,7:PRINT " Hit the space bar to continue ";:COLOR 7,0
730 A$=INKEY$:IF A$<>" " THEN 730
740 GOTO 150: REM *** Return to main menu ***
750 REM
760 REM *** Procedure to calculate prob that X less than some number ***
770 REM    ======================================================
780 REM
790 CLS
800 PRINT "Procedure to calculate probability that X less than a given value"
810 LOCATE 5,10:INPUT "Enter value of X";X
820 Z=(X-M)/S
830 IF Z=0 THEN RESULT=.5:GOTO 870
840 IF Z<0 THEN Z=Z*-1:H=1 ELSE H=0
850 GOSUB 60
860 IF H=0 THEN RESULT=1-PZ ELSE IF H=1 THEN RESULT=PZ
870 LOCATE 18,10:PRINT "Given a mean of ";M;" and a standard deviation of ";S
880 LOCATE 20,10:PRINT "the probability of X less than ";X
890 LOCATE 22,10:PRINT "is ";:PRINT USING ACC$;(INT(RESULT*ACC)/ACC)
900 LOCATE 24,25:COLOR 0,7:PRINT " Hit the space bar to continue ";:COLOR 7,0
910 A$=INKEY$:IF A$<>" " THEN 910
920 GOTO 150: REM *** Return to main menu ***
930 REM
940 REM *** Procedure to calculate prob that X lies between two values ***
```

```
950 REM       =============================================================
960 REM
970 CLS
980 PRINT "Procedure to calculate probability that X lies between two values"
990 LOCATE 5,10:INPUT "Enter low value of X";X1
1000 LOCATE 7,10:INPUT "Enter high value of X";X2
1010 IF X2>X1 THEN 1020 ELSE LOCATE 10,10:PRINT "Error - high value must exceed
low value":GOTO 990
1020 Z=(X1-M)/S
1030 IF Z=0 THEN PART1=.5
1040 IF Z<0 THEN Z=Z*-1:H=1 ELSE H=0
1050 GOSUB 60
1060 IF H=0 THEN PART1=PZ ELSE IF H=1 THEN PART1=1-PZ
1070 Z=(X2-M)/S
1080 IF Z=0 THEN PART2=.5
1090 IF Z<0 THEN Z=Z*-1:H=1 ELSE H=0
1100 GOSUB 60
1110 IF H=0 THEN PART2=PZ ELSE IF H=1 THEN PART2=1-PZ
1120 RESULT=PART1-PART2
1130 LOCATE 18,10:PRINT "Given a mean of ";M;" and a standard deviation of ";S
1140 LOCATE 20,10:PRINT "the probability that X lies between ";X1;" and ";X2
1150 LOCATE 22,10:PRINT "is ";:PRINT USING ACC$;(INT(RESULT*ACC)/ACC)
1160 LOCATE 24,25:COLOR 0,7:PRINT " Hit the space bar to continue ";:COLOR 7,0
1170 A$=INKEY$:IF A$<>" " THEN 1170
1180 GOTO 150:REM *** Return to main menu ***
```

8
An introduction to hypothesis testing

This chapter discusses the main ideas underlying hypothesis testing. In many ways this is the area of statistics that is of most interest to the businessman. We are concerned to test a particular hypothesis against an alternative to see which is the more likely to be true. Hypotheses may be tested on the basis of a variety of probability distributions. In later chapters we shall look at some alternative distributions which might be used but for the moment we shall use those distributions which have been introduced in the previous two chapters – the binomial and the normal – to explain the basic ideas. Nonetheless the *principles* discussed remain valid for all hypothesis tests and it is on these principles that this chapter concentrates. Various applications are presented in the succeeding chapters.

Introductory ideas

When considering a particular problem, we will have to define some aspect of it that we wish to test. For instance, suppose that a hotel runs a marketing campaign. There are a number of aspects that might be tested – for instance, was it successful, was it unnecessarily expensive, should it be repeated/continued? If we are to apply statistical reasoning to the testing of these different elements then we need to define them in such a way that they may be measured. Generally speaking this definition will emerge from the objectives of the marketing campaign. Of course the impact of some kinds of advertising/marketing may be more difficult to quantify than others but we should perhaps be wary of those who argue that the impact is impossible to quantify – do (or should) firms really spend profits on marketing campaigns where they have no way of assessing whether the results have been good, bad or indifferent? In some situations there may be no alternative, but in the majority of cases a company will have a good idea of what it wishes to achieve. More valid is the point of view which argues that testing is impossible because we are comparing what has happened with a marketing campaign against what might have happened in its absence, and of course we have no way of knowing the latter. This criticism should be directed however at decision-making in general rather than at the application of statistical methods since clearly the same problem is faced whatever method is used to evaluate a decision.

There seems little point in developing this kind of philosophical discussion further. All it really emphasizes is that decisions are difficult to make and evaluate, and that the more help that is available the better. Statistics is just one of many possible aids to improving decision-making; it is up to the user to decide whether it is useful or not in particular cases.

Let us continue a little longer with a marketing example. Suppose that we are advising a restaurant which is running a campaign with the aim of increasing the spend per cover. How are we to decide whether the campaign has been successful or not? One obvious way to proceed would be to compare the average amount spent per cover before the campaign with the average amount afterwards. However, this may run into problems of seasonality so that it may make more sense to compare average spend for the same period the previous year. In either case we shall be comparing two averages and in particular what will interest us is the difference between them.

If there is no difference or if the average spend is lower following the campaign, we are unlikely to conclude that it has been successful (unless there are special circumstances to take into account, for instance a strong downturn in the market). Normally we would expect the average spend to be greater after the campaign than it was before it. The problem now is to decide how much greater? For instance, suppose that the average spend before the campaign was £10.52 and that afterwards it is £10.53 – the average spend is greater, but we would almost certainly say that there is no real evidence in favour of the campaign. The reason for this is that intuitively we recognize that there is bound to be some variation in the average spend, with or without the campaign, so that a figure that is only slightly higher will probably be put down to this variation rather than to marketing.

If, on the other hand, the post-campaign spend had been £15.00 then we would almost certainly be convinced that the campaign had had the desired impact. The difficult thing is then to decide the cut-off point between deciding that the campaign has or has not worked. This cut-off point may be defined arbitrarily, without any use of statistical methods. We simply decide prior to (or even after) the campaign that a particular value, for example £11, is to be the critical value. If the average spend is more than this, then the campaign has worked; if it is less, then the campaign has not worked.

It will probably come as a great disappointment to some readers that statistics uses an equally arbitrary approach! The tester must decide what is a significant result and what is an insignificant one. Once again statistics does not provide right and wrong answers. More helpfully it does provide a method for calculating how likely you are to be right and wrong. In an uncertain situation this is the best that can be done.

In the next chapter we will return to this marketing problem and other applications. However, to explain the basic principles of hypothesis testing, the remainder of this chapter uses a simpler example so that we can test the logic of what we are doing. Once more we will try to emphasize that the approach taken is intuitively sound even if the methods occasionally seem a little obscure.

Basic terminology

When undertaking a statistical test the first thing that we require is a hypothesis which is to be tested. Generally speaking this hypothesis is set up in what might be called a negative way in the sense that if it is accepted then the status quo will obtain. It is the equivalent of the legal system wherein the accused person is assumed innocent until proven guilty.

This fundamental hypothesis is known as the *null* (nothing) *hypothesis* and is denoted as H_0. We need to compare our null hypothesis with some alternative. Generally this *alternative hypothesis* is denoted as H_1 or sometimes H_A. In the legal environment this alternative is of course that the person is guilty. It is interesting to note that the two hypotheses are mutually exclusive and complementary – one of the two has to be accepted, and this acceptance automatically results in the rejection of the other. Statistical tests also must be established in this way.

Consider a trivial but revealing example. Suppose that a friend gives you a coin that she says is biased (that is it comes down either heads or tails more frequently than it should). The obvious way to test this claim is to start tossing the coin, noting the outcomes. However it is not possible to continue indefinitely tossing the coin so you will have to fix a certain number of attempts, at least if you are to test the coin systematically. You will also need to make a decision as to how many heads or tails (or what proportion) are required before you will accept the claim of bias. Before doing any of this however you will have, implicitly at least, to establish a null and alternative hypothesis. Suppose that your friend is prone to exaggeration so that you do not believe her. Your implicit null hypothesis will be that the coin is *not* biased which you will test against an alternative that it is biased. The exact form of your alternative hypothesis will depend on what your friend has told you. If she has said that the coin is biased to heads then you will need to check whether you get too many heads. If, on the other hand, she tells you it is biased to tails, then you must check whether there are too many tails. Finally, if you are simply told that the coin is biased then you will have to watch out for both possible biases.

If you find that the above discussion seems somewhat obvious, then so much the better because it means that you have understood the fundamentals of establishing a hypothesis test. All statistical hypothesis tests are formulated in the same way: a null hypothesis is tested against one of three possible alternatives. Let us formalize a little the ideas discussed above.

The null and alternative hypotheses

Our null hypothesis is that the coin is unbiased. There are a number of ways that we could measure bias. For instance, if the coin is unbiased then we expect to get 5 heads and 5 tails if we toss it 10 times. Hence our null hypothesis could be that the number of heads (or tails) is 5 (assuming $n=10$). A more elegant way of saying the same thing is to consider the probabilities directly. No bias means that the probability of getting heads on each throw is 1/2 as is the probability of getting tails. This gives:

$$H_o : p(H) = 1/2$$

Our null hypothesis is that the probability of getting heads is one-half. If our statistical test (see following section) supports this hypothesis, then we will conclude that the coin is not biased.

The alternative hypothesis may take one of three forms. First, if it is suspected that the coin is biased towards heads, then the probability of getting a head on any one toss will be greater than a 1/2. Hence, the alternative hypothesis will be:

$$H_1 : p(H) > 1/2$$

Secondly, if bias is suspected towards tails then the alternative hypothesis will be:

$$H_1 : p(H) < 1/2 \ (=> P(T) > 1/2)$$

Finally, where there is no indication of the direction of bias prior to the
test, all that can be said is that if the coin is biased then the probability of
getting heads on a single toss will not equal 1/2. The alternative hypothesis then becomes:

$$H_1 : p(H) <> 1/2$$

The statistical test

For the sake of argument, we will suppose that we are testing for bias to
heads. We have then two mutually exclusive hypotheses (they cannot
both be true at once). We now require a quantitative method (that is, a
statistical test) for deciding which is the more likely to be true.

Such a test might be that we toss the coin 60 times. If we get 37 heads,
what are we to conclude? The first thing to notice is that our sample size is
relatively small. Some people might suggest as a first step increasing the
size of the sample. However, although such an approach would be
feasible here, as we have noted previously, business (and other) experiments are often expensive and/or difficult to replicate so that using small
samples may be difficult to avoid.

One obvious conclusion that can be drawn is that the coin is not biased
towards tails (on the evidence that we have). At least, therefore, the
hypothesis test seems correctly formulated. However, we must still
choose between bias to heads or no bias. On the face of it bias to heads
seems the most logical conclusion. The difficulty in accepting this lies in
the fact that *even if the coin is not biased* there is some probability that we
would get 37 heads in 60 throws. The advantage of a statistical approach
is that we can calculate this probability and thereby find the probability
that our conclusion is incorrect.

Two kinds of error

As you should by now recognize, the above problem is binomial in
nature. Using the binomial probability distribution, we can find the
probability of getting 37 heads in 60 tosses of an unbiased coin. That is,
we proceed on the assumption that the null hypothesis is true.

The basic parameters of the distribution are: $n=60$, $p=0.5$, and $q=0.5$.
We can easily find the probability of obtaining 37 heads. However, if 37

heads means that the coin is biased to heads then logically we would also have to conclude that the coin were biased if we obtained 38 or more heads. Summing these various probabilities (using for example the normal approximation to the binomial) gives the probability of concluding that the coin is biased when, in fact, it is not. In such a case, we would reject the null hypothesis, H_o, when it is true. This is generally called a *type-I error* (occasionally it is referred to as type-alpha).

If in the above example we use 37 heads as our cut-off point (i.e. 37 or more heads = biased to heads; 36 or less = not biased to heads) then the size of the type-I error is 0.04623, that is about 4.6%. Thus if the coin is NOT biased there is a 4.6% chance of getting 37 or more heads and hence a 4.6% chance of making a type-I error. The values of the variable for which the null hypothesis is rejected are known collectively as the *rejection region* and the values for which it is accepted as the *acceptance region*.

It should be apparent that we can easily reduce the chances of making a type-I error by reducing the size of the rejection region. For example, we might decide to accept that the coin is biased to heads only if we get 40 or more heads. Now the chance of making a type-I error is only 0.67%, which seems to be a much better result.

Unfortunately there exists a second possible source of error in our tests called naturally enough a *type-II error*. This is when we accept the null hypothesis as being true when in fact it is false. Hopefully it is apparent that if we reduce the size of the rejection region then we increase the chances of making a type-II error at the same time as we reduce the chances of making a type-I error. We are forced to make a trade-off between the two kinds of error.

Table 8.1 summarizes the possible outcomes of a hypothesis test.

Table 8.1   *Possible outcomes of a hypothesis test*

	H_o *accepted*	H_o *rejected*
H_o true	Correct decision	Type-I error
H_o false	Type-II error	Correct decision

There are no hard and fast rules for determining the size of the acceptance and rejection regions (and hence the size of the type-I and type-II errors). It depends on the problem under consideration. Consider, for example, the famous case in the UK where a train was driven at great speed into a reinforced concrete container used for dumping nuclear waste. The null hypothesis here is clearly that the containers are safe. A test is performed to check this against the alternative hypothesis that they are not safe. The consequences of accepting the null when it is false (type-II error) are potentially cataclysmic in this case and the rejection region should therefore have been as 'large' as possible (we will consider in detail in a moment what might constitute 'large' in the context of hypothesis testing). If we increase the size of the rejection region then we increase the chances of making a type-I error (i.e. rejecting the null when it is true – in this case we would conclude that the containers were not safe when in fact they were). In this particular case it seems infinitely preferable to make a type-I error rather than a type-II and we should adjust the rejection region accordingly.

Perhaps fortunately most business decisions do not have such potentially disastrous consequences and therefore we tend to set the rejection region on the low side. For instance in the case of our marketing example, if the rejection region is small then the chances of us concluding that the campaign is successful when in fact it is not are reduced. Thus further expenditure on such a campaign would only be made if the campaign was really having an effect. This strategy does mean that the type-II error is increased – on some occasions a successful campaign will be halted – but this is likely to be preferred to a situation where large sums are spent on ineffective campaigns. Of course not everyone may agree with such a strategy and it may not be appropriate at all times. The important thing to note is that you cannot avoid the problems of type-I and type-II errors but you can choose the value that they are to have by altering the strategy that you or your firm are following. This is a significant advantage in decision-making situations.

So far we have established the size of the rejection region (and thereby the acceptance region) using particular values of the test statistic, and we have then calculated the probability of observing these values if the null hypothesis were true – this probability being the type-I error.

One-tailed tests

The more usual approach is to start with the size of the type-I error that is felt to be appropriate to the problem under consideration and then to work back to find the corresponding value of the test statistic. One of three values is generally taken as the size of the rejection region – 0.01 (or 1%), 0.05 (5%) and 0.1 (10%). If we can reject the null hypothesis with a rejection region of only 0.01 then the result is said to be significant at the 1% level – there being only a 1% chance that we have made a type-I error. Generally such a result is said to be 'highly significant'. If the null can only be rejected with a rejection region of 0.05 then the result is significant at the 5% level only and is said to be 'significant'. Finally, if the result is only significant at the 10% level then it is 'probably significant'. Generally the significance level of a test is denoted by the Greek letter, α, alpha (which is why the type-I error is also called type-alpha).

One common approach in statistics is to choose one of the three significance levels prior to conducting the test and then to make a decision according to the results obtained. An alternative, perhaps more common in academic literature, is to conduct the test and then report what is the smallest rejection region at which the result is significant. It is then left to the user of the study to decide if this level of significance is adequate for action to be taken.

In the coin-tossing example above, we have effectively already applied the second approach. If we obtain 37 heads from 60 tosses of the coin, then we could report the results as being significant at the 4.6% level. Alternatively, using the three cut-off values cited above, we could say that the test is significant at the 5% level but not at the 1% level. To some extent, however, this approach dodges the issue since if a decision is to be taken someone must decide what is the critical level of significance.

If we adopt the approach of specifying the rejection region prior to conducting the test, how do we proceed? First, we must decide on the critical level of significance. Suppose that we decide on 1%. We must now work back and find the value of the variable (here, the number of heads) which gives this probability of making a type-I error.

In this problem, the values of np and nq are large enough to justify use of the normal distribution. We are used to the idea of going from a binomial version of a problem to the normal and thence to the standard normal. This time we must make the reverse journey. We know that the probability of making a type-I error must be 1% (i.e. 0.01). What we must find is the value of Z in the standard normal which corresponds to this probability. That is:

$$P(Z > a) = 0.01$$

We must find the value of a. As usual, a number of methods may be used to find this value. The simplest and most commonly-employed method, however, is simply to use the tables which exist for this purpose. In Murdoch and Barnes these are presented as Table 4 (p.14) 'Percentage points of the normal distribution'. These tables give the probability value in the left-hand column and the corresponding Z-value (called in the tables a u-value) in the right-hand column. Looking at these tables, we can see that a probability of 0.01 corresponds to a Z-value of 2.3263. Generally these values are taken as accurate to 2 decimal places so that this value becomes 2.33. The other frequently-used significance levels, 0.05 and 0.1, correspond to Z-values of 1.65 and 1.28 respectively. Once you have done a little work in hypothesis testing you will come to know these values by heart.

We know then that a 1% significance level corresponds to a Z-value of 2.33. We must now translate this value back into the original normal distribution. To do this we make use of the equation used to standardize a normal distribution. When we have the original X-values, we standardize using the equation:

$$Z = \frac{x - \mu}{\sigma}$$

which rearranging implies that:

$$x = \mu + Z\sigma$$

We know that a binomial distribution has mean $n \times p$ and standard deviation $\sqrt{(n \times p \times q)}$. In this example, n is 60, and p and q both equal one-half. Hence the mean is 30 and the standard deviation 3.873.

The X-value (number of heads) corresponding to a Z-value of 2.33 is therefore found as:

$$x = 30 + (2.33 \times 3.873) = 39.024$$

The final step is to express this value in binomial terms. This time we do not need to worry about adding or subtracting halves; we merely round the X-value to the nearest whole number.

In this case, if we decide to use a 1% significance level, then the critical number of heads will be 39. If we obtain this number or more then we will conclude that the coin is biased to heads; if not we will accept the null hypothesis of no bias.

This discussion is summarized in Figure 8.1. The rejection region is located entirely in the right-hand tail of the normal curve – hence the name one-tailed test. The test statistic lies just inside the acceptance region if a critical Z-value of 2.33 is used to separate the acceptance and rejection regions.

Testing for bias to tails would also be a one-tailed test. The procedure is exactly as before. We set up our null and alternative hypotheses:

$$H_o : p(H) = 0.5$$
$$H_1 : p(H) < 0.5$$

We then decide on a significance level, for example 5% which gives a critical Z-value of −1.65. We then sketch this area as in Figure 8.2. Next we calculate our test statistic, which for the sake of argument we will leave as 37 heads in 60 tosses of the coin.

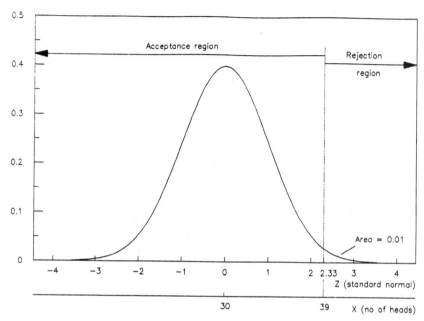

Figure 8.1 *A one-tailed test (upper test)*

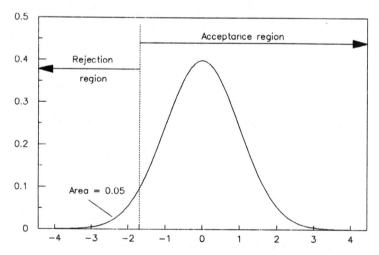

Figure 8.2 *A one-tailed test (lower test)*

We then either standardize the test statistic so that it is comparable with the critical Z-value, or we 'de-standardize' the critical Z-value so that it is comparable with the test statistic. It makes no difference which we do. The usual approach, however, is to standardize the test statistic using the general equation:

$$Z = \frac{x - \text{mean}}{\text{standard deviation}}$$

where in this case:

$$\text{mean} = np = 30$$
$$\text{s.d.} = \sqrt{npq} = 3.873$$

Using this equation we obtain 1.81 as our standardized test statistic. Clearly therefore we can accept H_o; the coin does not seem to be biased to tails.

One difficulty that students sometimes have with hypothesis tests is knowing in which tail of the normal curve the rejection region should be located. There is a simple solution to this problem. If your hypothesis test is correctly formulated then the inequality sign in H_1 acts as a kind of arrow pointing to where the rejection region should be.

A two-tailed test

If we have no reason prior to the test to suspect bias in one direction or the other then we need to check for bias both to heads and to tails. Our null and alternative hypotheses become:

$$H_o : p(H) = 0.5$$
$$H_1 : p(H) <> 0.5$$

Notice that the 'arrows' now point to either side indicating, correctly, that two rejection regions are required. If we want to have an overall significance level for the test of 0.5 (5%) then we locate 0.025 in each tail. Hence we have two critical Z-values, these being in this case plus and minus 1.96. The acceptance and rejection regions are then as shown in Figure 8.3.

The remainder of the test is conducted exactly as before. We calculate our test statistic and see whether it lies in the acceptance region or in one of the two rejection regions. We then decide whether to accept or reject H_o.

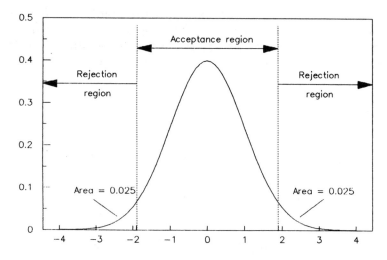

Figure 8.3   *A two-tailed test*

Summary of hypothesis test procedure

For any hypothesis test, the basic procedure is the same. What changes is the precise method used for calculating the test statistic, and the acceptance and rejection regions. This procedure may be summarized in the following five steps.

1   Establish the null and alternative hypotheses.
2   Decide on a significance level for the test.
3   On the basis of 1 and 2 establish acceptance and rejection regions for the test.
4   Calculate the test statistic.
5   On the basis of 3 and 4, reach a conclusion regarding H_o and H_1.

Note that when presenting the results of your test in step 5, always give the reader as much information as possible. In particular try to avoid simply saying that the hypothesis is not significant at, for instance, the 1% level. There is a lot of difference between a hypothesis that is not significant at 1% but is at 2%, and a hypothesis that is not significant even at 30%. Do not therefore present your results as if they were the same.

Conclusion

This chapter has used a trivial example as a means of introducing the principles of hypothesis testing precisely so that we could concentrate on the principles without having to worry about the application. Now that these basic principles have been mastered we can apply them in the following chapters to the kinds of problem facing decision-makers in the hotel and catering industry.

Exercises

1 Formulate the null and alternative hypotheses in the following situations:

(a) to test whether a majority of people favour an issue;

(b) to test whether average turnover in hotel 1 is less than that in hotel 2;

(c) to test whether there is any difference between weekly occupancy rate before and after a marketing campaign;

(d) to test whether the mean salary is greater than £200.

2 Classify the above into one- and two-tailed tests. Explain the difference between the two tests.

3 On your advice the manager of the hotel conducts a hypothesis test on a particular issue. The test is one-tailed and the standardized Z-value comes out as -2. How would you explain the fact that the result is significant at the 5% level but not at the 1% level?

4 Is a statistically significant difference necessarily an important one?

9
Hypothesis tests concerning means and proportions

The previous chapter introduced the basic ideas used in statistical hypothesis testing. In this chapter we shall apply these ideas to some problems concerning means and proportions. We begin by looking at tests involving means. Before we can do this, however, we need to consider briefly the idea of the sampling distribution of the mean. Fortunately, this is the final theoretical construct required before we reach the applications.

The sampling distribution of the mean

This idea is best explained via an example. Suppose that we have a very small statistical population which is made up of the following nine values:

$$2, 3, 3, 4, 4, 4, 5, 5, 6$$

The population mean is easily found as 4 and the population standard deviation as 1.16. The distribution is depicted in Figure 9.1.

If we did not know all these values and we wished to estimate the population mean then of course we would proceed in the usual manner, taking a random sample from the population and calculating its mean. This would give us an estimate of the population mean subject to an unknown error. However, via the sampling distribution of the mean, an idea of the likely size of this error can be calculated.

Samples may be taken with or without replacement. The latter has the advantage of effectively making the population infinite, but it cannot always be applied – for instance, where sampled objects must be tested to destruction. It is easier to understand the logic of the sampling distribution of the mean in the case where sampling is without replacement, and we will assume that this method is used.

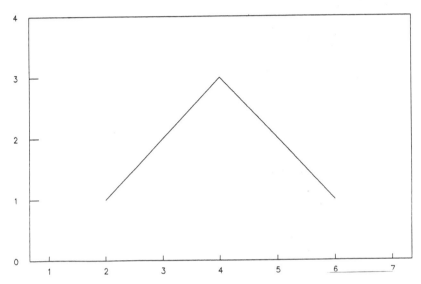

Figure 9.1   *A simple symmetrical population*

Suppose that a sample of size two is taken. If we calculate the sample mean, the smallest possible value that can be obtained is 2.5 (if our sample contains the two and a three) and the largest value is 5.5 (sample 5 and 6). If then we were to take many samples successively and graph the results, the curve would have to be less spread out than the curve describing the original data set. It would still centre on 4 but would have a higher peak because there are now many more ways to obtain a value of 4 (samples 2,6; 4,4; 3,5; etc.). This curve, which in fact has a plateau, is shown in Figure 9.2(a) for all possible samples of size 2.

If the sample size were increased to three, the smallest sample mean would become 2.67 (sample 2, 3, 3) and the largest 5.33 (5, 5, 6). Hence the distribution of sample means would be even more tightly packed (as in Figure 9.2(a).

With sample size 4, the smallest sample mean is 3 and the largest 5. Thus as we increase the sample size, the possible error involved in using the sample mean as an estimate of the population mean declines. Figure 9.2 demonstrates this for sample sizes 2 to 8. Separate graphs are required because the number of possible samples increases with the sample size (in accordance with the equation for a permutation). Nonetheless, it is clear, as would be expected, that the sample mean becomes a better estimator of the population mean as n increases.

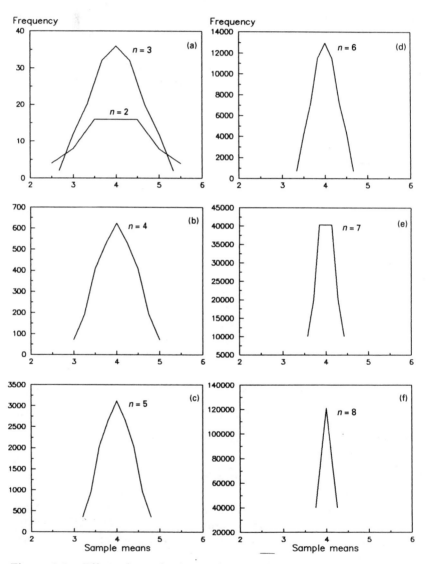

Figure 9.2   *Effect of sample size on the spread of sample means around the population mean*

In addition to the sample size, the spread of sample means around the population mean will depend on the population variance: the more spread is the original data set, the more spread will be the sample means. In the example, suppose that we add one value to the population. If this value is 25 then the population variance is increased. It is intuitively clear that the spread of sample means is also increased since occasionally a sample will contain the 25. If, on the other hand, the added value is a 4 then the population variance falls and so does the spread of sample means since we add yet more ways in which a sample may be constructed whose mean exactly equals the population mean.

The variance of the sample mean thus depends on two factors – the population variance, σ^2, and the sample size, n. The precise relationship is:

$$S_x^2 = \sigma^2/n \tag{9.1}$$

where S_x^2 is the variance of the sample means. If we square root this variance then we obtain, as always, the standard deviation of the sample means. However, this particular standard deviation has been baptized the *standard error of the mean*. Do not let this confuse you, it is a standard deviation like any other whatever it may be called. We have then:

$$s_x = \sigma/\sqrt{n} \tag{9.2}$$

Strictly speaking, this equation applies only in cases where the population is infinite. In almost all business applications this will be the case. If however the population is finite, a correction (called the *finite population correction factor*) must be applied to the standard error, giving:

$$s_x = (\sigma/\sqrt{n}) \times \frac{N-n}{n-1} \tag{9.3}$$

where N is the population size and n is the sample size.

If this correction is not used the estimate of the standard error is too great. For example, in the limiting case, if the sample size is the same as the population then there will be no standard error since the sample mean will always have the same value. This result will be obtained if the correction factor is used but not otherwise since Equation (9.2) will give a positive result.

The term *sampling distribution of the mean* refers then to the distribution or graph of sample means. Two results may be derived from this sampling distribution that are very important in hypothesis testing.

1   If we have a normal population with mean, μ, and variance, σ², and random samples of size *n* are taken, then the sample means will also be normally distributed with mean, μ and variance, σ²/*n*.

2   Even more usefully, an important statistical theorem, the *central limit theorem* (CLT), states that if we have a population with *any* distribution with mean, μ and variance, σ² then the sample means will be normally distributed, *provided* that *n* is sufficiently large. In practice, a value of 30 is generally sufficient.

The central limit theorem seems too good to be true. It says that regardless of the structure of your basic data set, means calculated from samples taken from it will be normally distributed so long as the samples are large enough. If you find this theorem difficult to believe or grasp, test it for yourself. Set up a population, for example using a set of random number tables, and take (largish) samples from it. Calculate the means of these samples and plot them on a graph. If the theorem is correct (which it is) and if your samples are large enough (which they might not be) then your sample means will follow approximately a normal distribution. (Note that it is almost essential to use a computer to take a random sample and calculate the means. Writing a small program that does this is not too difficult and is a good exercise for your computing course.)

The two results 1 and 2 presented above are extremely important for many of the hypothesis tests involving the mean.

Hypothesis tests concerning the mean

Having introduced the idea of the standard error of the mean, we can finally turn to the application of hypothesis tests. We will begin by looking at tests concerning mean values. The construction of tests follows the method explained in Chapter 8.

A hotel chain knows from its records that weekly turnover in one of its hotels has averaged £228,512. One year ago, a new manager was appointed with the objective of improving this figure. Over the past 52 weeks, turnover has averaged £240,854 with a standard deviation of £42,156. From this evidence, can we conclude that the new manager has been associated with a real (i.e. statistically significant) increase in turnover; or is the change in the average figure merely due to chance factors?

Setting up the null hypothesis on a no-change basis (as usual) against an alternative hypothesis that the turnover has increased gives:

$$H_0: \mu = 228{,}512$$
$$H_1: \mu > 228{,}512$$

As the sample size (number of weeks) is relatively large, we can invoke the central limit theorem, that is the sample mean is normally distributed. We can also use the sample variance to approximate the population variance. Hence probabilities may be calculated using the standard normal distribution. To do so, we must first standardize our values. This standardization is done exactly as before:

$$Z = \frac{x - \text{mean}}{\text{standard deviation}}$$

except that here the standard deviation is given by the standard error. Hence

$$Z = \frac{x - \mu}{\sigma / \sqrt{n}} \approx \frac{x - \mu}{s / \sqrt{n}} \tag{9.4}$$

The Z-value corresponding to the test statistic is then found to be:

$$Z = \frac{240{,}854 - 228{,}512}{42{,}156 / \sqrt{52}} = 2.11$$

Either now or perhaps at an earlier point we must decide on the size of the rejection region. If we want to be as sure as possible that the increase in average value is not a fluke then we should set a level of significance such as 1%. Since we have a one-tailed test, a probability of 0.01 corresponds (from Table 4 of Murdoch and Barnes, p. 14) to a critical Z-value of 2.33. At this level of significance we cannot be sure that the result is not due to luck and therefore we are unable to reject H_0. However, if we were to accept a 5% level of significance then the critical Z-value would become 1.65. In this case we would reject H_0 and accept H_1 that the new manager was indeed associated with an increase in average weekly turnover. The chances of making a type-I error would be 5% – i.e. there is a chance that the underlying (or population) average weekly figure has not changed.

One final point should be noted. We can test how likely it is that changes in variables are statistically significant. We can also associate such changes with changes in other variables (e.g. a new manager). What we cannot do is prove that there is a causative link. The new manager may be associated with an increase in weekly turnover without necessarily being the cause of it. There may be many reasons why turnover increases (e.g. inflation), which are totally independent of who is the manager. Of course, in many cases the results of a statistical test will be used precisely to infer such causation. Where the results are supportive, as above, most managers are more than happy that this should be the case. Given this, they cannot perhaps complain if a poor performance is used against them. The problem of association of events and causation is a difficult one which pervades much of statistics.

Hypothesis tests concerning proportions

In many situations we do not have the exact values of variables but only know the proportion of cases in which some event occurs. We can also conduct tests concerning such proportions. Consider the case of the binomial distribution.

We know that as n increases the binomial is approximately normally distributed with mean, n multiplied by the probability of success, and variance, mean multiplied by the probability of failure. Strictly we should use the population probability of success, π, in the standardization of X. Where, however, π is not known it may be replaced by the sample probability, p, provided that np and nq ($q=1-p$) are both greater than 5 (as we saw in Chapter 6). A given value of a binomial random variable, X, is standardized to Z using the equation:

$$Z = \frac{x - n\pi}{\sqrt{[n\pi(1-\pi)]}} \qquad (9.5)$$

If instead of knowing the value of x, we simply know the proportion of times that it occurs then we have the value x/n. Dividing all terms on the right-hand side of the equation by n leaves the value of Z unchanged, but gives the useful result:

$$Z = \frac{x/n - \pi}{\{\sqrt{[n\pi(1-\pi)]}\} / n} = \frac{x/n - \pi}{\sqrt{[\pi(1-\pi) / n]}} \qquad (9.6)$$

That is, the binomial proportion is also approximately normally distributed.

Suppose that a catering company takes delivery of an order for 10 tonnes of potatoes. Due to the perishable nature of the product, the company knows that a certain proportion of the order will be spoiled and unusable. From experience and after discussion with the supplier it has been agreed that the company will qualify for a rebate if more than 3% of the potatoes (by weight) are spoiled on the day of delivery (the supplier takes no responsibility for the storage of the potatoes awaiting use). Upon delivery the quality control department of the company takes a random sample of 500 kilogrammes of potatoes, of which 19.5 are found to be spoiled. Does this evidence confirm that the 3% threshold has been crossed?

The hypothesis test is set up in the usual way. Our null hypothesis here is that the population proportion (denoted as π) of spoiled potatoes is 3% (0.03) which we will test against the alternative that it is more than 3%.

$$H_o : \pi = 0.3$$
$$H_1 : \pi > 0.3$$

The test statistic is the proportion of potatoes found to be spoiled in the sample, i.e. 19.5/500 = 0.039. We will suppose that the company wants to be reasonably sure before calling in the supplier and therefore the test will be undertaken at the 1% significance level. As we know, the critical Z-value for this level of significance is 2.33.

If H_o is true we can apply equation (9.6) with π=0.3 giving a calculated Z-value of:

$$Z= \frac{0.039 - 0.03}{\sqrt{(0.03 \times 0.97 / 500)}} = 1.18$$

On the basis of the random sample taken, the null hypothesis cannot be rejected at the 1% level (nor in fact at the 10% level) and the company should therefore accept the order as being of the agreed quality.

Hypothesis tests concerning the difference between two means

So far we have considered tests concerning the value of a mean or a proportion. Often however it is of more interest to consider the difference between two values. We will consider first the case of two means.

We saw in the first section of this chapter that the sample mean of a random variable X will be normally distributed *provided* either that X itself is normally distributed or that the sample size n is sufficiently large (30 or more).

Suppose now that we consider two populations (1 and 2) and that we take samples from each. We then calculate the difference between the sample means for given sample sizes, n_1 and n_2. If both sample means are normally distributed then it should not come as a surprise that the difference between them is also normally distributed. Since $\bar{x}_1$ is an estimate of μ_1 (the population mean) and $\bar{x}_2$ is an estimate of μ_2 then again it is to be expected that the difference between the sample means will centre on the difference between the population means. Finally, the spread of the difference between the sample means will depend on the spread of sample mean 1 plus the spread of sample mean 2. In fact to obtain the variance of the difference between the means we have simply to add the individual variances. These results are extremely useful for conducting hypothesis tests. They may be formalized as follows:

If X_1 and X_2 are two random variables coming from two populations 1 and 2 and $\bar{x}_1$ and $\bar{x}_2$ are sample means based on n_1 and n_2 observations respectively then

$$(\bar{x}_1 - \bar{x}_2) \text{ is } N(\mu_1 - \mu_2, \sigma^2_1/n_1 + \sigma^2_2/n_2)$$

provided that X_1 and X_2 are normally distributed or n_1 and n_2 are large.

Suppose that a restaurant chain has been running a marketing campaign with the goal of increasing the average spend per cover. As a check on the results a random sample of 250 covers was taken immediately before the campaign began. This sample showed that the average spend was £11.23 per cover with a standard deviation of £3.65.

Following the campaign a second random sample of 200 covers is taken. This sample reveals an average spend per cover of £13.21 with a standard deviation of £2.89.

Given the evidence available, what are we to conclude about the marketing campaign?

As usual we must first establish our hypothesis and rejection region. The null hypothesis here is that there is no real difference between the two sample means (i.e. the two sets of data on which they are based come from the same population). This hypothesis is usually written as:

$$H_0: \mu_1 - \mu_2 = 0$$

Equivalently, it is sometimes written as:

$$H_0: \mu_1 = \mu_2$$

The alternative hypothesis is that the marketing campaign has been successful and therefore the population of amounts spent per cover is greater after the campaign than it was before it. This gives:

$$H_0: \mu_1 - \mu_2 < 0$$

We must now calculate our rejection region. Let us suppose that the campaign has been tried in a test area and that the chain wants to be sure of the results before extending it to other areas. For this reason, it is decided to test at the 1% level. Notice that the rejection region is located in the left-hand tail giving a negative critical Z-value of −2.33.

We now calculate our test statistic, which here is the difference between the two sample means. Since both n_1 and n_2 are large, the central limit theorem tells us that this difference will be normally distributed. We then standardize in the normal way, even if here the resulting equation appears a little complicated. In general we have:

$$Z = \frac{\text{test statistic} - \text{mean}}{\text{standard deviation}}$$

Substituting in the appropriate quantities gives:

$$Z = \frac{(x_1 - x_2) - (\mu_1 - \mu_2)}{\sqrt{(\sigma^2_1/n_1 + \sigma^2_2/n_2)}} \approx \frac{(x_1 - x_2) - (\mu_1 - \mu_2)}{\sqrt{(s^2_1/n_1 + s^2_2/n_2)}} \qquad (9.7)$$

$$= \frac{(11.23 - 13.21) - (0)}{\sqrt{(13.3225/250 + 8.3521/200)}} = -6.422$$

The calculated Z-value clearly lies well inside the rejection region so that H_0 is rejected. On the basis of the available evidence, the chain may safely extend the marketing campaign to other areas.

Hypothesis tests about the difference between two proportions

In some cases, rather than working with the actual or mean values of a variable, it may be easier or more useful to consider the proportion of successes. Once again the discussion is based on the binomial and the normal approximation to it.

The derivation of the test of the difference between two proportions is similar to that of the test of the difference between two means. We know from Equation (9.6) that the proportion of successes (x/n) is normally distributed with mean, π, and variance, $\pi(1-\pi)/n$.

If we consider two populations then the difference between the proportion of successes, $x_1/n_1 - x_2/n_2$, will also be normally distributed with mean, $\pi_1 - \pi_2$, and variance, $\pi_1(1-\pi_1)/n_1 + \pi_2(1-\pi_2)/n_2$.

The application of these results to a hypothesis test is almost exactly the same as before. Suppose for example that a hotel believes its occupancy is running at 10 percentage points above that of the opposition. Over a 5-night period, it checks occupancy levels for itself and its major competitors. It finds that for itself, it sold 684 out of 900 potential roomnights. The competition meanwhile according to the data that the hotel has been able to accumulate sold 2188 out of 3150 available. Does the evidence support the hotel's belief concerning its lead in occupancy?

Once more we begin by establishing our basic hypothesis. The null hypothesis is that the difference between the proportion of successes is 10 percentage points. This gives:

$$H_0 : \pi_1 - \pi_2 = 0.1$$

In this case we do not know whether the opposition have been doing better or worse and so we need to test both cases. Consequently we should use a two-tailed test, where half of the rejection region is located in each tail of the normal distribution. Hence the alternative hypothesis is simply that the difference is not 10%, i.e.

$$H_1 : \pi_1 - \pi_2 <> 0.1$$

We next establish the size of the rejection region. In this case let us use the standard 5% significance level which, since half is located in each tail, gives two critical Z-values of $+1.96$ and -1.96. If the test statistic lies between these limits we accept H_0 otherwise we reject it.

Our test statistic becomes:

$$Z = \frac{(x_1/n_1 - x_2/n_2) - (\pi_1 - \pi_2)}{\sqrt{[\pi_1(1-\pi_1)/n_1 + \pi_2(1-\pi_2)/n_2]}} \qquad (9.8)$$

Since, however, these are not known the sample values will be used to estimate them: this procedure being justified by the large sample sizes. Substituting in for the various values in Equation (9.8) gives:

$$Z = \frac{(684/900 - 2190/3000) - (0.1)}{\sqrt{[(0.76 \times 0.24 / 900) + (0.73 \times 0.27 / 3000)]}} = -4.332$$

Given the calculated value of Z the null hypothesis is rejected. On the basis of the data available, the hotel does not seem to have a 10 percentage point lead in occupancy over its competitors.

Where the hypothesis to be tested concerns a stated difference between the two proportions the test should be established exactly as in the example. Often however we will be interested simply in whether there is a difference between the two proportions. In this case the null hypothesis is written as follows:

$$H_o : \pi_1 - \pi_2 = 0 \text{ (or equivalently } \pi_1 = \pi_2)$$

As in the previous case, the population proportions will not generally be known and must be estimated via the samples. The difference is that this time, assuming that H_o is true, both sample proportions are estimates of the same value (since $\pi_1 = \pi_2$). Rather than using the two estimates separately, a better result is obtained if they are combined into a single overall estimate of the population proportion. This is done by summing the successes and summing the sample sizes, and is written:

$$\pi = \frac{x_1 + x_2}{n_1 + n_2} \tag{9.9}$$

This value replaces π_1 and π_2 in the denominator of Equation (9.8). The remainder of the equation remains unchanged.

Continuing the example above, suppose that the hotel having found that it does not have a 10 percentage point lead now wishes to test whether it has any lead at all. The null hypothesis is that the two proportions are equal against the alternative that the hotel is doing better. These hypotheses are written as:

$$H_o : \pi_1 - \pi_2 = 0$$
$$H_1 : \pi_1 - \pi_2 > 0$$

Our test statistic is now:

$$Z = \frac{(x_1/n_1 - x_2/n_2) - (0)}{\sqrt{[\pi(1-\pi)/n_1 + \pi(1-\pi)/n_2]}}$$

From Equation (9.9) we have:

$$\pi = \frac{684 + 2190}{900 + 3000} = 0.7369$$

The calculated value of Z is then given as:

$$Z = \frac{(684/900 - 2190/3000) - (0)}{\sqrt{[(0.7369 \times 0.2631/900) + (0.7369 \times 0.2631/3000)]}} = 1.79$$

Testing again at the 5% level the critical Z-value is found to be 1.65. The null hypothesis is therefore rejected: the hotel does seem to have a higher occupancy rate than its competitors even if the lead is not 10 percentage points.

Small sample tests

So far this chapter has discussed the testing of a number of statistical hypotheses concerning means and proportions. In most management-type situations these tests will be sufficiently accurate to guide decision making. However, perhaps the biggest stumbling block with the tests introduced so far is that we have to assume (or better know) that we are dealing with a normal population or alternatively that we have a large sample so that the central limit theorem may be invoked. In this section, we introduce some statistical tests that have been developed for the case where only a small sample is available.

In many practical situations large samples are impossible or prohibitively expensive to collect. In such cases, statistical tests based on, for instance, the normal distribution tend to be unreliable at the margin. An alternative distribution, developed by WS Gossett (who published under the pseudonym 'Student'), is the t-distribution, this being specifically designed to deal with small samples.

The t-distribution

The t-distribution shares many of the characteristics of the normal distribution. First, it is based on a standardized variable (which is t rather than Z). Second, the curve describing the distribution is centred on a standardized value of zero. Third, the curve is symmetrical about this value.

The great innovation with the t-distribution is that the size of the sample is taken into account so that there is a different t-curve for each possible sample size. As the sample size increases the t-distribution becomes increasingly normal. For small sample sizes, however, the t is flatter than the normal so that more of the area is found in the tails of the distribution. Consequently, with a small sample the critical t-value will be higher than the critical Z-value. In other words, more evidence will be required before H_o is rejected.

The sample size is taken into account via the concept of 'degrees of freedom'. The calculation of degrees of freedom depends on the case being considered. The general idea may be explained using the example from the first section of this chapter. Consider a particular sample mean value such as 3.5. If the sample is of size 2, then once the first observation has been chosen there is obviously only one other value that will give the correct answer. For example if our first value is 4 then the other one has to be 3, otherwise we will not get the mean that we require. If we increase the sample to 3, then choosing a first value of 4 does not fix the other two values. We have also to know the second value and then the third one is determined for us. If the sample is size 4 then we need to know three values to fix the fourth. As is evident the number of 'degrees of freedom' is one less than the sample size in this case.

The t-curve depends directly on the number of degrees of freedom and hence indirectly on the sample size. Although there is a different t-curve for each level of degrees of freedom, the general shape is as shown in Figure 9.3. Tables of probabilities exist for the t-distribution. The use of these tables is exactly the same as for the normal distribution. The only difference is that in addition to the significance level of the test, we need also to know the number of degrees of freedom to be able to calculate the critical t-value to determine the acceptance and rejection regions. Murdoch and Barnes (Table 7, p. 16) give critical t-values for different

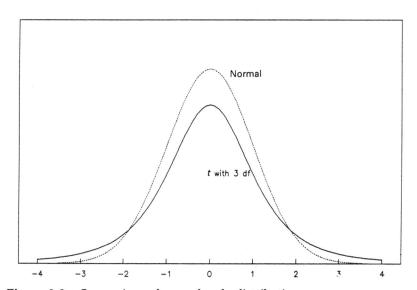

Figure 9.3 *Comparison of normal and t distributions*

significance (α) levels and for different degrees of freedom (denoted by the Greek letter, ν).

A small sample hypothesis test of the mean

Hypothesis tests using the t-distribution follow exactly the same method as previous tests introduced in this chapter. Consider, for example, the following problem.

Nine months ago, a hotel chain opened a new unit. Average monthly turnover was targeted to be £300,000 after a two month settling-in period. The hotel manager is worried that results indicate that the target is not being met. The turnover figures for the last seven months (in thousand pounds) are as follows: 327, 258, 269, 318, 280, 262, 301. Given these results is the manager right to be worried?

We can establish a hypothesis test of the mean as before. In this case, we have:

$$H_0 : \mu = 300,000$$
$$H_1 : \mu < 300,000$$

The sample mean is £287,587.14 and the sample standard deviation is £27,661.21. Since we have a small sample, we use the t-distribution. The test statistic is the same as with the normal distribution:

$$t = \frac{\bar{x} - \mu}{s / \sqrt{n}} \tag{9.10}$$

Substituting the above values into this equation gives a calculated t-value of -0.166.

The critical t-value depends on the significance level of the test. Suppose that we test at 5%. We have six degrees of freedom ($n-1$). From the t-tables, the critical t-value is -1.943 (negative because we have a one-tailed test in the lower tail of the distribution). Clearly the calculated t-value lies well inside the acceptance region – the hotel's results so far are consistent with it achieving an average turnover of £300,000 per month.

Note that in this case the (strictly speaking, incorrect) use of the normal distribution would have led to exactly the same conclusion since the critical Z-value at a 5% significance level is -1.65. In this case also we would have accepted H_0. The use of the t-distribution makes results more accurate at the margin (i.e. where we are close to the critical level).

Small sample tests of the difference between two means

The *t*-distribution is often used to test whether there is a significant difference between the mean values of two samples. Two cases can be distinguished: one where we have two independent samples, and the other where we have paired values (for instance, the occupancy of each hotel in a chain considered separately before and after a marketing campaign).

Independent samples

In the two independent samples case, the purpose of the test is to discover whether the two population means are equal or not. This may be interpreted in one of two ways. First, we might test whether the two samples come from the same population. Second, we might test whether they come from two different populations.

In the first case, if H_0 is true then the two (unknown) population variances will be equal. The advantage of this is that information in the two samples can be pooled to provide a single estimate of the population variance. For this reason, this case is known as the *equal (or pooled) variance* case. If however we are unable to justify this assumption then we have to estimate each population variance separately via the appropriate sample. This is the *separate variance* case. The *t*-distribution was originally developed in the former case. The latter is however the more general and it should be used if there is doubt. As we shall see the difference between the two tests lies only in the way in which the degrees of freedom are calculated.

Whichever case is considered, the test is constructed in the usual way.

$$H_0 : \mu_1 - \mu_2 = 0$$
$$H_1 : \mu_1 - \mu_2 <> 0 \text{ (or } >0 \text{ or } <0)$$

The test statistic is essentially the same as we had in the case of the normal distribution:

$$t = \frac{(\bar{x}_1 - \bar{x}_2) - (\mu_1 - \mu_2)}{\sqrt{(s^2_1/n_1 + s^2_2/n_2)}} \tag{9.11}$$

In the *equal variance* case both s_1 and s_2 are estimates of the same σ. We could use either of them in the formula for the test statistic but as is to be expected a better estimate of σ is obtained if we combine the information from the two samples. This is known as a pooled estimate of σ. The pooled estimate is calculated as a weighted average of the two sample estimates (the weights being the degrees of freedom associated with each sample). Hence

$$s^2{}_p = \frac{(n_1 - 1)s^2{}_1 + (n_2 - 1)s^2{}_2}{n_1 + n_2 - 2} \qquad (9.12)$$

Consider for instance the following example. A hotel group offers various room rates. It decides to test whether a policy of top-down selling produces worse occupancy figures than bottom-up selling. It implements the first policy in 8 of its hotels and the second policy in the remaining 5. Average occupancy in the first group is 62% with a standard deviation of 4.2%. In the second group, occupancy is 75% with a standard deviation of 8.6%. Does the top-down policy worsen occupancy? (Prior to the test occupancy levels were roughly the same in the two groups.)

If we assume that the two samples are normally distributed and that they have similar variances then we can use the t-test described above. First, as always, we establish our hypothesis test. Here it is:

$$H_0 : \mu_1 - \mu_2 = 0$$
$$H_1 : \mu_1 - \mu_2 < 0$$

Next we calculate our test statistic on the assumption that H_0 is true. We begin by pooling the data available on the common variance, which applying Equation (9.12) gives:

$$s^2{}_p = \frac{(8-1)4.2^2 + (5-1)8.6^2}{8+5-2} = 38.12$$

Once we have this value, we can calculate t using Equation (9.11). We obtain:

$$t = \frac{(62-75) - (0)}{\sqrt{(38.12/8 + 38.12/5)}} = -3.69$$

Once again the critical t-value will depend on the level of significance and the number of degrees of freedom. Suppose we set α at 0.01 (1%). In this case, we lose one degree of freedom for each sample so that the total will be the sum of the two sample sizes minus 2, i.e.

$$df = n_1 + n_2 - 2 = 8 + 5 - 2 = 11$$

given $\alpha = 0.01$ and 11 degrees of freedom, the critical t-value is found from the tables to be -2.718.

Clearly therefore the calculated t-value lies in the rejection region. Hence we reject H_o, on the basis of the data available, a top-down selling policy seems to decrease average occupancy.

If the assumption of equal population variances is untenable then we use a slightly modified test. Provided that the sample sizes are similar, the assumptions of normality and equal variances can be violated without invalidating the results of the test. Where the two variances are not equal (or where we do not know if they are equal or not) a modified t-test is used. The number of degrees of freedom is now calculated according to the formula:

$$v = \frac{[s^2_1/n_1 + s^2_2/n_2]^2}{[(s^2_1/n_1)^2 / (n_1-1)] + [(s^2_2/n_2)^2 / (n_2-1)]} \qquad (9.13)$$

The value obtained from this equation is used in the calculation of the degrees of freedom. It is probable that the result will not be a whole number, in which case the answer is simply rounded. The major difference between the two methods is that the number of degrees of freedom is reduced in the second case. This reduction compensates for the violation of normality and/or equal variance assumptions. It is important to note, however, that in cases where these assumptions are far from being met, the compensation is inadequate and a different statistical test would have to be used (for example, chi-squared or another non-parametric test – such tests are discussed in Chapter 11).

Applying Equation (9.13) to the previous example gives a value of 5.215 which rounds to 5 degrees of freedom (compared with the 11 that we had previously). For the given significance level of 1%, the critical t-value becomes -3.365. While in this case we would still be able to reject H_o it is clear that the assumption of equal variances is an important one.

A test does exist (the F-test) to check for equality of variance. Unfortunately, it turns out that this test is much more sensitive to departures from normality than the t-test. As a result, one well-known statistician has said that using the F-test to check whether the t is appropriate is like sending an ocean liner to check whether the sea is calm enough for a yacht. We shall not bother further therefore with this test. Where in practice you are not sure, the separate variance test should be used. In this way only significant results will be identified (at the possible cost of an unnecessarily large type-II error).

Paired samples

In some situations, rather than just comparing the mean value of two sets of data it is more revealing to pair the data points in some way and then consider the differences between the pairs. For example, suppose that a hotel employs two chefs. Their work is of similar quality so the hotel manager would like to assign them to the tasks that they do fastest. Before upsetting the established regime however she wishes to check whether one of the two is not simply a faster worker than the other over the whole range of dishes prepared. Simply testing the mean time taken to prepare a dish will not work because the results will be biased by the fact that some dishes take longer than others. An alternative therefore is to consider the difference in time taken for each dish.

Suppose then that a discrete study of the two chefs gives the results contained in Table 9.1.

Table 9.1 *Time taken by two chefs to prepare various dishes*

Dish	Chef 1	Chef 2	Difference
A	24	31	−7
B	7	5	2
C	14	18	−4
D	9	10	−1
E	34	30	4
F	22	29	−7
G	8	11	−3

What are we to make of this data? In fact, we now simply conduct a small sample test of a mean. The only difference from the earlier small sample test is that since the data points are paired, we work with the differences rather than with values. We set up a null hypothesis as usual. In this case, it is that there is no real difference between the chefs, the observed differences being due to chance. We test this against an alternative, that one of the two is a speedier worker (since we do not know which, we have a two-tailed test – in practice, of course, the manager may well have sufficient suspicion to make this a one-tailed test). We have then:

$$H_0 : \mu_d = 0$$
$$H_1 : \mu_d <> 0$$

The test statistic will have the usual general form:

$$t = \frac{x - \text{mean}}{\text{standard deviation}}$$

In this case the x is the mean of the sample differences and the standard deviation is the standard error of this mean. Hence the test statistic is:

$$t = \frac{\bar{x}_d - \mu_d}{s_d / \sqrt{n}} \tag{9.14}$$

From the difference column of Table 9.1, the mean and standard deviation of the differences are found to be -2.286 and 4.231 respectively. Substituting these values into Equation (9.14) gives:

$$t = \frac{-2.286 - 0}{4.231 / \sqrt{8}} = -1.53$$

(Note: n is here the number of pairs of observations.)

Testing at the 5% level with 7 degrees of freedom, the critical t-values for a two tailed test are plus and minus 2.365. The test statistic clearly lies in the acceptance region. On the basis of the data available, there is no reason to suppose that one chef is a consistently speedier worker than the other.

Conclusion

In this chapter we have seen that a variety of methods exist for testing different hypotheses. However, what the chapter has tried to emphasize is that the logic underlying these tests is always the same. We calculate a test statistic and then use probability theory to check how likely we are to obtain such a result if the null hypothesis is true. All of the tests introduced in this chapter have as their base the simple probability theory introduced in Chapter 4. The reason why there are many tests is that first, there are many situations that we may wish to test, and second, from experience, it has been found that some tests are unreliable in particular situations (notably the normal distribution with small samples) and so other methods have been introduced to calculate the probabilities in these situations.

In the next chapter we use the results derived here to look at two more important issues – first, that of giving a range of values within which, say, the mean is likely to lie and second, that of determining how large a sample needs to be taken.

One drawback with the tests discussed here is that they require that a summary measure of the population be calculated. Sometimes however such a measure may be impossible or meaningless to calculate. In such cases a different set of hypothesis tests have been developed that consider the data set as a whole rather than summary measures of it. These tests are discussed in Chapter 11.

Exercises

1   The management of a hotel claims that average salary is £500 per wek. Trade union officials doubt that this can be true. They conduct a survey, taking a random sample of 150 workers from the group. They find a mean salary of £465 per week with a standard deviation of £20.

   Do these findings support or contradict the management claim?

2   The manager of a fast-food outlet feels that service times are too slow. He decides therefore to employ 3 extra staff. A study of service times gives the following results.

Time taken	Frequency
Less than 10 seconds	6
10 – < 20	18
20 – < 30	28
30 – < 40	35
40 – < 50	30
50 – < 60	17
60 – < 70	12
70 – < 80	10
80 and over	3

   If average service time had previously been calculated at 42.7 seconds what is to be concluded regarding the impact of the three new staff?

3   A hotel bar decides to implement a 'happy hour' to try to improve bar takings. Previously, a sample of 20 days had given a mean takings of £650 per day with a standard deviation of £75. Now that the happy hour has been running for a while, a sample of 17 days gave mean takings of £680 with a standard deviation of £45.

   On the basis of these data what can be concluded about the impact of the happy hour on bar takings?

4   A tour company attempts to control the quality of service given by its hotels by using the number of complaints received. However, in

normal circumstances it still expects to get 5% of its guests complaining about something. If at a hotel, 10 out of 150 guests complain, is the service adequate or inadequate?

5   A canning machine is supposed to produce tins with an average weight of 498.5 grammes. A sample of 250 tins is taken revealing a mean of 498.2 grammes with a standard deviation of 0.18 grammes. What conclusion can be reached about the machine?

6   A hotel has introduced a new policy designed to reduce the number of no-shows. Previously the number of no-shows was 8%. Over a two-month trial period the number of no-shows has fallen to 6%. Does this mean that the new policy is a success?

10
Confidence intervals and sample size estimation

In previous chapters we have concentrated on the problem of obtaining an estimate of a population mean or proportion from a given sample. We know, however, that there is almost no chance that the population and sample values will coincide exactly, due to the problem of sampling error. An alternative approach therefore is to attempt to determine a range of values within which the true population value is likely to be found. This range is called a *confidence interval*.

In addition to being useful in their own right, confidence intervals also allow a calculation to be made concerning the size of sample required to limit the sampling error to a particular value. We shall begin by looking at the determination of the confidence interval.

Confidence intervals: the confidence interval for the mean

A confidence interval is derived directly from the logic already developed in previous chapters. Take for example the case where we have a large sample on the basis of which we are trying to estimate the population mean. We know (Chapter 9) that the sample mean will be normally distributed with mean equal to the population mean and variance equal to the population variance divided by the sample size. As the population variance is generally unknown, it tends to be estimated by the sample variance.

Suppose that we now wish to test the null hypothesis that the population mean is equal to a particular value against the two-tailed alternative that it is not equal to this value. We calculate a standardized test statistic,

Z. Depending on the significance level set for the test, critical Z-values are established which determine a rejection and an acceptance region for H_o.

In terms of the notation adopted in the earlier chapters we have the following:

$$H_o : \mu = 0$$
$$H_1 : \mu <> 0$$

The standardized Z value is:

$$Z = \frac{\mu - \bar{x}}{\sigma / \sqrt{n}} \approx \frac{\mu - \bar{x}}{s / \sqrt{n}}$$

If H_o is true then we have (for a given level of significance α):

$$-Z_{\alpha/2} < Z < +Z_{\alpha/2} \tag{10.1}$$

This inequality corresponds to the acceptance region. If the value of Z lies beyond the critical Z-values in either direction then we reject the null hypothesis.

The inequality (10.1) may be rearranged to provide a confidence interval for μ. If we substitute Z by its definition then we have:

$$-Z_{\alpha/2} < \frac{\mu - \bar{x}}{\sigma / \sqrt{n}} < +Z_{\alpha/2}$$

and rearranging we obtain:

$$\bar{x} - [Z_{\alpha/2} \times (\sigma/\sqrt{n})] < \mu < \bar{x} + [Z_{\alpha/2} \times (\sigma/\sqrt{n})] \tag{10.2}$$

This inequality is the confidence interval for μ. We can see that the interval will depend on the sample size, the sample mean and the population standard deviation (or its sample equivalent if the population value is unknown). Once these values have been determined, it will also depend on the significance level. For this reason, an indication of the α-value is given. The general case derived above is said to be the $(100-\alpha)\%$ confidence interval. Hence if α is set at 5% then we have a 95% confidence interval; at 1%, a 99% interval and so on.

The application of the interval is straightforward. Suppose for example that a hotel is looking at the average length of stay. A sample of 250 bills reveals a sample mean of 2.54 nights with a standard deviation of 0.82.

The 95% confidence interval for the true population mean is then found using the inequality (10.2). The critical Z-values are plus and minus 1.96. Hence we have:

$$2.54 - [1.96 \times (0.82/\sqrt{250})] < \mu < 2.54 + [1.96 \times (0.82/\sqrt{250})]$$

which gives a 95% confidence interval for the mean of between 2.49 and 2.59 nights.

Changing the α-value changes the size of the confidence interval. For example the 99% confidence interval (critical Z-values plus and minus 2.58) is between 2.41 and 2.67 nights – that is, as would be expected, a wider interval is required if we wish to be more sure that it contains the true mean.

The interpretation of the confidence interval

The interpretation of the confidence interval poses something of a problem. The accepted interpretation in statistics is as follows. In a given situation, the true (unknown) population mean has a particular value, for instance 2.48. The limits calculated for the confidence interval also have given values. For instance, in the case of the 95% limit above the values are 2.49 to 2.59. Since all three values are given, the confidence interval either does or does not (as in this case) contain the mean. We cannot therefore say that the *probability* is 0.95 that the mean lies between the given limits.

The strict interpretation of a 95% confidence interval is that if we take many samples and calculate a 95% interval for each sample then, on the average in the long run, 95% of the intervals will contain the mean and 5% will not. However, each interval taken on its own either will or will not contain the mean, as shown in the previous paragraph.

The problem with this interpretation is that in practice only one sample is likely to be available. For the concept to be useful therefore it has to be interpreted in a probability sense. In other words we have to use the interval as if there were, for example, a 95% probability that the true mean lies somewhere within it. Moreover, such an interpretation does not seems unjustifiable. We do not know the true mean (otherwise we would not be trying to estimate it) but we know that if we take random samples and calculate confidence intervals based on them, 95% of such intervals contain the true mean. If we select one such interval at random there must therefore be a 95% chance that the one chosen contains the mean.

This is not the place to develop a discussion of the problem of defining a confidence interval. Suffice it to say that whatever theoretical interpretation is given to it, the practical application of the confidence interval is clear. It gives an estimate of upper and lower values for a parameter, such as the mean. These limits may be more useful to management than a simple estimate of the most likely value. Working at the lower limit may help to avoid for example the problem of overbooking.

Some other confidence intervals

In the same way that the hypothesis test about the mean can be re-arranged to give a confidence limit, so may the other hypothesis tests discussed earlier. In this section we will briefly look at some other confidence intervals that may be derived.

First, a confidence interval may be established for the case where we are estimating *the mean from a small sample*. Z is then replaced by *t*. The critical *t*-values depend on the significance level (α) and the number of degrees of freedom (v). Otherwise the confidence interval is the same as above (10.2), giving:

$$\bar{x} - [t_{\alpha/2,v} \times (s/\sqrt{n})] < \mu < \bar{x} + [t_{\alpha/2,v} \times (s/\sqrt{n})] \qquad (10.3)$$

The following example indicates how this interval may be applied. Ten months ago, a hotel bought a second-hand ice-making machine for use in its bar. Unfortunately, this machine has proven somewhat temperamental, breaking down quite frequently. The hotel technician can usually repair the fault relatively quickly. However, to cope with breakdowns, a stock of ice is kept. The barman knows that ice consumption is roughly 7 litres per hour. It is decided to keep in stock a quantity of ice sufficient to last for the length of time represented by the upper bound of the 99% confidence interval for the average breakdown. During the last ten months the machine has broken down a total of 7 times. The average length of breakdown has been 2 hours with a standard deviation of 45 minutes. How much ice should be stocked?

We have a small sample and we will assume that the breakdown times are normally distributed in which case the *t*-distribution may be used. Since we have a sample of size 7, we have six degrees of freedom. A 99% confidence interval ($\rightarrow \alpha/2 = 0.005$) gives critical *t*-values of plus and minus 3.707. In this case we are in fact only interested in the upper value. Substituting into Equation (10.3) we have:

$$\mu < 120 + [3.707 \times (45/\sqrt{7})] = 183.05$$

In other words the upper bound for the population mean length of breakdowns is 3 hours 3 minutes. Since the bar uses 7 litres of ice per hour, 21.35 litres should be stocked.

Second, a confidence interval may be derived for the case where we are estimating the *population proportion* based on the normal approximation to the binomial. The standardized test statistic:

$$Z = \frac{x/n - \pi}{\sqrt{[\pi(1-\pi)]/n}}$$

is standard normally distributed. Rearranging it in the same way as with inequality (10.2) gives the confidence interval for π as:

$$x/n - \{Z_{\alpha/2} \times \sqrt{[\pi(1-\pi)]/n}\} < \pi < x/n + \{Z_{\alpha/2} \times \sqrt{[\pi(1-\pi)]/n}\} \qquad (10.4)$$

This interval might be applied in the following problem. A hotel manager is trying to determine the proportion of guests who arrive more than 3 hours late compared to their expected time of arrival. A sample of 200 guests reveals 3.5%. Construct the 95% confidence interval for the true proportion who are this late.

Substituting the values into Equation (10.4) gives:

$$0.035 - [1.96 \times \sqrt{(0.035 \times 0.965)/200}] < \pi < 0.035 - [1.96 \times \sqrt{(0.035 \times 0.965)/200}]$$

hence:

$$0.01 < \pi < 0.06$$

In other words, given the findings in the sample the true figure for 3-hour late arrivals lies between 1% and 6%.

Third, a confidence interval for the *difference between two means* can be constructed using analogous methods. We know (Chapter 9) that the test statistic:

$$Z = \frac{(\bar{x}_1 - \bar{x}_2) - (\mu_1 - \mu_2)}{\sqrt{(\sigma^2_1/n_1 + \sigma^2_2/n_2)}}$$

is standard normally distributed provided that either the underlying populations are themselves normal or the samples are large (over 30). Rearranging gives the confidence interval as:

$$(\bar{x}_1 - \bar{x}_2) - [Z_{\alpha/2} \times \sqrt{(\sigma^2_1/n_1 + \sigma^2_2/n_2)}] < \mu_1 - \mu_2 < (\bar{x}_1 - \bar{x}_2) + [Z_{\alpha/2} \times \sqrt{(\sigma^2_1/n_1 + \sigma^2_2/n_2)}] \qquad (10.5)$$

Although this interval may look complicated, its application is again straightforward.

Consider the following example. A food manufacturer is testing two kinds of packaging machinery. The makers of machine A claim that it results in an average of 75 packets rejected per production run compared to 110 with machine B; this difference being sufficient to justify the higher price of machine A. Tests of the two machines give the following results. Machine A had an average of 82 rejects per production run over 55 runs with a standard deviation of 15. Machine B had an average of 115 rejects per production run over 60 runs with a standard deviation of 20. Establish the 95% confidence interval for the true difference between the two machines.

Substituting the test values into inequality (10.5) gives:

$$(82-115)-[1.96\times\sqrt{(225/55+400/60)}]<\mu_1-\mu_2<$$
$$(82-115)+[1.96\times\sqrt{(225/55+400/60)}]$$

hence

$$-36.28<\mu_1-\mu_2<-29.72$$

With 95% confidence, the difference between the population means lies between 29.72 and 36.28 rejects in favour of machine A. This interval is consistent with the claims made by the machine's manufacturer and would seem to justify its purchase.

A confidence interval for *the difference between two means based on small samples* may easily be constructed from inequality (10.5) using the *t*-distribution as was the case with the small sample mean. The construction of this interval is left as an exercise.

Sample size determination

Confidence intervals may also be used to give a guide to the question: how large a sample should be taken? Before looking in detail at the method, let us briefly consider the problem in principle.

In conducting an experiment, one approach would be to consider every possible outcome. For example, we could contact every possible potential customer of our hotel and ask for their opinions regarding the topic under consideration. This approach is called taking a census. In practice however this is generally impossible because of the difficulty in identifying all the people involved and the cost of contacting them. As a result a sample is selected. The sample also involves a cost, however, comprising two parts – that of contacting members of the sample and that due to the loss of accuracy in the results as compared with a census. The optimal sample size is the one that minimizes the sum of these two costs, *provided* that this sum is less than the cost of a census. For very important decisions, the costs of potential errors might be so great that a census is the most cost-effective solution. Generally however a sample will provide acceptably accurate results at lower cost particularly in a business environment.

The great difficulty with applying the principle of sample size determination as elaborated above is the problem of estimating the cost involved in sample error. Because of this, the principle is generally not applied directly. Instead an approximation suggested by confidence intervals is used.

Consider, for example, the problem of determining the population mean. We decide on a level of sampling error that is tolerable. This error will be in terms of the original units and should represent a value that is considered 'important' by the tester (or the person asking for the test). Obviously the less is the error that is acceptable, the greater will have to be the sample size, other things being equal. In other words, given the difficulty of estimating μ precisely, we will have to be prepared to accept μ plus and minus an error (e). We know therefore that our result should have the following quality:

$$\bar{x} = \mu \pm e \text{ and hence } \mu = \bar{x} \pm e \tag{10.6}$$

For the moment, let us express the acceptable error in terms of the confidence interval. Suppose that we decide that a 99% confidence interval is acceptable. This implies, as we know, critical Z-values of plus and minus 2.58. We know from inequality (10.2) that:

$$\bar{x} - [Z_{\alpha/2} \times (\sigma/\sqrt{n})] < \mu < \bar{x} + [Z_{\alpha/2} \times (\sigma/\sqrt{n})]$$

Combining this inequality with (10.6), it is obvious that the error must be given as:

$$e = Z_{\alpha/2} \times (\sigma/\sqrt{n})$$

hence

$$\sqrt{n} = (Z_{\alpha/2} \times \sigma) / e$$

and

$$n = [(Z_{\alpha/2} \times \sigma) / e]^2 \tag{10.7}$$

Consider again the estimation of the average length of stay introduced in the first section of this chapter. Assume that σ is 0.82 and that we wish to limit the error to 0.1 (that is we wish to estimate the average length of stay to within 1/10th of a day). What sample size should be taken?

Using Equation (10.7) we obtain:

$$n=[\ (2.58 \times 0.82)\ /0.1\ ]^2=447.58$$

Hence if we wish to limit the error in the estimate to 0.1 with 99% confidence a sample of 448 bills should be taken. The fact that the sample taken above was less than this (only 250 bills were used) accounts for the greater error, the spread of values being 0.13 either side of the estimated mean.

If, as is so often the case, σ is unknown then we have a problem since Equation (10.7) will contain two unknowns σ and *n*. Since we are interested in determining *n*, some estimate of σ must be obtained. Generally, an adequate working estimate can usually be found either from a previous study of the same phenomenon or from a similar study conducted elsewhere. If, however, new ground is being broken then a pilot study will have to be undertaken to estimate σ prior to conducting the complete survey. It makes sense, however, to make as good a guess as possible of σ prior to conducting the pilot study since, if you are lucky, the sample will turn out to be sufficiently large for a follow-up to be necessary.

A similar procedure is followed in the case of proportions. The error around the population proportion is given as:

$$e=Z_{\alpha/2} \times \sqrt{(\pi(1-\pi)/n)}$$

Rearranging we obtain:

$$\sqrt{n}=(Z_{\alpha/2} \times \sqrt{\pi(1-\pi)})\ /\ e$$

Hence:

$$n=(Z^2_{\alpha/2} \times \pi(1-\pi))\ /\ e^2 \tag{10.8}$$

As in the previous case, an initial value for π might be available from a previous or similar study. Alternatively, π can simply be set to 0.5 to begin with. This method represents what might be called a safety-first strategy in that of all the possible values of π, 0.5 is the one giving the largest *n*. However, if π is very different to 0.5, the strategy will result in an unnecessarily large and perhaps expensive sample being taken. It is preferable therefore to attempt to obtain some idea of π before starting wherever this is possible.

As an application of Equation (10.8) consider again the example presented earlier in this chapter concerning the population proportion. At present, the error is 0.025 either side of the best estimate of 0.035. Suppose that the manager wishes to limit the error to 0.01 with 95% confidence, what size sample should be taken?

Using equation (10.8) we obtain:

$$n=(1.96\times(0.035\times0.965))\ /\ 0.01^2 = 661.99$$

Hence to limit the error to this amount would require an increase in the sample size from the 200 presently used to 662.

If we had no prior information regarding the likely proportion and we used the 0.5 rule then the necessary sample would become:

$$n=(1.96\times(0.5\times0.5))\ /\ 0.01^2 = 4900$$

As can be seen, although it will always work, the use of this rule may result in unnecessary expense. In this case it seems clear a-priori that the proportion of guests who are more than 3 hours late has to be a relatively small number so that setting an initial p-value at say 0.2 would seem a reasonable compromise. In most cases some indication of a starting value for p exists. As the example above shows, it is usually worth using any available information.

Optimal sample sizes in other situations may be determined in a similar manner.

Conclusion

In this chapter, we have seen how it may be preferable to provide a range of values within which a population parameter is likely to be found rather than simply providing the best single estimate. We have also seen how such a range may be used to decide upon the size of sample that must be taken.

In some situations, however, it may be difficult or even meaningless to try to calculate population parameters. For example, merely because 50% of a hotel's guests are male and 50% female does not mean that the average guest is a hermaphrodite. In such situations rather than working with different parameters to try to resolve statistical hypotheses, it may make more sense to work directly with the data set. It is to the study of such tests that the next chapter turns.

Reference

An example of confidence intervals being applied and used to determine sample size is provided by:

GULLEN, H. and RHODES, G. (1983), *Management in the Hotel and Catering Industry*, Batsford, see Chapter 9, especially pp. 110–14.

Exercises

1   A sample of 150 bills from the hotel coffee shop gives a mean of £2.23 with a standard deviation of £0.87. Construct the 95% confidence interval for the true average per bill in the coffee shop.

　　How would the interval change if the above results had been based on a sample of only 15?

2   A hotel restaurant manager would like to know the proportion of guests arriving who are likely to wish to take dinner. A random sample of 75 guests gives 28% who wish to dine. Construct the 99% confidence interval for the true proportion.

　　The manager is very disappointed by your answer and would like to know the true figure to within ±2%. How large a sample would have to be taken to obtain this result?

3   A food manufacturer is considering purchasing a new control system to reduce the number of tins that are rejected as underweight at the quality control stage. Over the past 1000 production runs, the mean number of tins rejected was 25 with a standard deviation of 5. It is expected that the variability of the new system would be similar but the mean number of rejects would be reduced.

　　Due to the expense of the new system, it is decided that it will be adopted only if its performance is significantly better at the 99% level. In a trial involving 100 production runs, what is the maximum average number of rejects that would be acceptable if the machine is to be purchased?

11
The chi-squared distribution and other non-parametric tests

The hypothesis tests introduced in previous chapters conduct a test around a given parameter of the population. For example, we may test whether the population mean is equal to a particular value. Such tests are consequently called *parametric*. One difficulty with parametric tests is that they generally require that certain assumptions regarding the population or populations be met. For example, in the case of the t-distribution, we saw that for the results of a test of the difference between two means to be valid, it is necessary that the underlying populations be normally distributed. Often it is very difficult, if not impossible, to verify this assumption and some statisticians argue that as a result t-tests are frequently used in situations where they should not be. On the other hand, experiments have shown that the results obtained tend to be *robust* (i.e. they remain correct) in the face of minor deviations from normality.

Rather than assuming away the problems or relying on the robustness of the tests, however, other statisticians have sought to develop tests that do not require such assumptions. This class of test works directly with the sample data set rather than with parameters calculated from it. Such tests are therefore said to be *non-parametric*. The best known non-parametric test is the chi-squared (denoted by the Greek letter x^2 - pronounced 'ky' as in 'sky'). We begin this chapter with a discussion of this test. We then briefly consider some other tests. Too many such tests have been devised for a comprehensive review to be possible here and only a few examples are presented. The interested reader is referred to further reading at the end of the chapter.

Non-parametric tests have both advantages and disadvantages compared to their parametric counterparts. On the positive side, they avoid, as we have said, the need to investigate the population distribution. They also allow tests to be undertaken regarding qualitative variables. On the other hand, they are less powerful than parametric tests, by which is meant that for a given sample size and a given type-I error, a type-II error is more likely with a non-parametric test. Many non-parametric tests are also less efficient in the sense that they utilize less of the information contained in the sample than do parametric tests. Notwithstanding such disadvantages, the ability to apply non-parametric tests to all kinds of situation has led to enormous interest in their application and new tests are continually being developed. In most business situations, since life and death does not usually depend on the results of hypothesis tests, non-parametric methods are often sufficiently accurate.

The chi-squared test

The chi-squared test is based on a comparison of the data which are observed in practice and those which would have been expected on the basis of probability theory. A null hypothesis is established exactly as with other hypothesis tests. Two main tests are undertaken using chi-squared – one to test whether a data set has a particular distribution, the other to test whether two data sets are independent of one another.

In both cases the procedure is similar. We establish a null hypothesis of the form that the data do NOT conform to the distribution or that the data sets are NOT dependent on one another (i.e. that they are independent). We then calculate the values that we would expect to obtain if the null hypothesis were true and compare these with the values observed in practice. If there is a difference between the two then we would reject the null. As always the problem is that some (relatively small) differences may be put down to chance. The difference must therefore be one that is *statistically significant*. This is where the x^2 distribution has an important role to play.

As was the case with previous hypothesis tests, a critical value of x^2 is established so as to define the acceptance and rejection regions. A value of x^2 is then calculated from the data and according to the results obtained the null is then accepted or rejected.

The test statistic (the calculated value) is derived as follows. We are interested in the difference between the observed values (0) and those which are expected (E). For each value of the variable, we calculate this difference $(O-E)$

We then wish to obtain an idea of the difference between the O and E values for the data set as a whole. An obvious procedure would be simply to add up the individual differences in $(O-E)$. However, as will become clear from the examples below, we run into the same problem that we had with the spread of values around the mean – namely that over the whole data set the values are symmetrical and sum to zero. Previously we avoided this problem by squaring and the same solution is adopted here – i.e. we consider the values $(O-E)^2$.

There is one final problem, however, and once again this is similar to the spread of values around the mean. Suppose that we simply add up the squared differences between O and E and we obtain a value of 80. This may indicate a significant difference if the observed values are in the tens but it probably would not if they were in the millions. In other words we again need some way to standardize the calculated values. The method used is to express the squared difference as a proportion of the expected value. Hence for each value of the variable we calculate, $(O-E)^2/E$. We then add up these values for the whole data set. This gives the equation for calculating x^2 as:

$$x^2 = \Sigma \ \frac{(O-E)^2}{E} \tag{11.1}$$

There is only one point that must be remembered in the calculation of x^2. The *expected* value at each level must always be at least 5. If it is not classes must be combined until the adjusted class has an expected value of 5 or more.

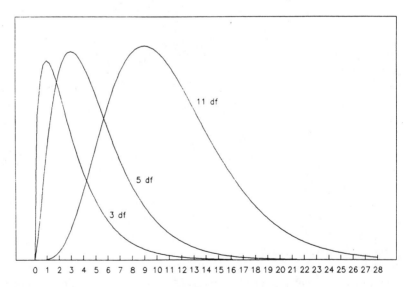

Figure 11.1 *The chi-squared distribution*

The critical x^2 value depends, like the t-test, on the significance level of the test plus the number of degrees of freedom. The calculation of degrees of freedom depends on the particular case being considered. However, the concept of degrees of freedom is very important since it determines the shape of the x^2 distribution (see Figure 11.1). Frequently, the curve for 5 degrees of freedom is presented as 'the chi-squared distribution' and if you have already come across this distribution you may have seen this curve. However, as shown in Figure 11.1, the shape changes with the degrees of freedom and as their number increases, the x^2 approaches a normal distribution.

As with the other probability distributions, tables of x^2 probabilities exist (Murdoch and Barnes, Table 8, p. 17). The use of these tables is exactly the same as for the t-tables discussed in Chapter 9.

Having looked at the general ideas underlying the x^2 test, we now turn to some applications.

Chi-squared tests of goodness of fit

In a test of goodness of fit, we hypothesize that the data are being generated by a particular process – for example, that each outcome is equally likely, that they follow a normal distribution, that they follow a binomial distribution, etc. We compare the data obtained with those which we would expect on the basis of probability, assuming the null hypothesis is true. Obviously this test can usefully be applied in situations where we are unsure as to the structure of the basic population and where we wish to apply a hypothesis test.

We can test either a general hypothesis – of the form, is the population binomial? – or a more specific one – such as, is the population binomial with $p=0.35$?

The conduct of the test is the same as with other hypothesis tests. Four main steps have to be taken:

1 Formulate hypotheses H_o and H_1.
2a Define the significance level of the test (α).
2b Calculate the degrees of freedom (df). In a goodness of fit test, df is given as follows:
   $$df = no. of classes - 1 - no. of parameters to be estimated$$
2c Hence determine critical x^2 value.
3 Calculate the value of x^2 which will be used as the test statistic.
4 Compare the critical x^2 value with the test statistic, and decide whether H_o should be rejected or accepted.

The great advantage of the x^2 test is that it can be used to test any distribution, not just those such as normal and so on. This is extremely useful particularly in business where many probability distributions are empirically determined.

Suppose, for instance, that a restaurant changes its menu from time to time as a result of customer surveys. Customers are asked about their satisfaction with various aspects of the menu and on the basis of their answers are classified into one of five possible groups. These groups are labelled: very satisfied, satisfied, indifferent, dissatisfied, and very dissatisfied. These surveys are conducted at regular yearly intervals and at other times if management feels that a problem is developing. The hotel statistician compares the results of the previous test with that of the current one to see whether there has been a significant change in customer attitudes to the menu.

The results of the last and current test are presented in Table 11.1. On the basis of the data available, have attitudes changed?

The null hypothesis is established in the usual way, that there has been no change, and is tested against the simple alternative that there has been a change. Hence:

$$H_0 : \text{attitudes unchanged}$$
$$H_1 : \text{attitudes changed}$$

It is decided to test this at the 5% significance level. The last two classes will have to be combined because the number of observations is too small (expected value less than 5). Consequently, there are 4 classes left which gives 3 degrees of freedom. From Table 8 in Murdoch and Barnes (p.17) we can see that the critical x^2 value is 7.815. In other words if the calculated value is less we accept H_0 otherwise we accept H_1.

Table 11.1   *Customer responses to menu*

Category	Last test	This test
Very satisfied	28	15
Satisfied	151	140
Indifferent	74	85
Dissatisfied	15	16
Very dissatisfied	1	2

The calculated x^2 value is found from Equation (11.1). To apply this equation, we need to calculate the expected values. If H_0 is true then the proportion of people in each category should not have changed since the last survey. We can calculate, therefore, the expected values by multiplying the number of people included in this survey by the proportion found each category in the last. This procedure gives the expected values shown in Table 11.2:

Table 11.2 *Observed versus expected values in a goodness of fit test*

Category	Last test	This test	Expected	$O-E$	$(O-E)^2$	$(O-E)^2/E$
Very satisfied	28	15	26.86	−11.86	140.66	5.24
Satisfied	151	140	144.83	−4.83	23.33	0.2
Indifferent	74	85	70.97	14.03	196.84	3
Dissatisfied	15	16)	15.35	2.65	7.02	0.5
Very dissatisfied	1	2)				
	269	258				$\Sigma=8.9$

We then apply Equation (11.1), calculating first $(O-E)$, squaring the result and dividing by E. The calculated x^2 values comes out as 8.9. Comparing this with the critical x^2 value, we find that the calculated value lies in the rejection region. On the basis of the data available, attitudes to the menu have changed since the last survey.

The great advantage of the x^2 distribution is that any kind of probability distribution may be tested using it. We do not have to assume that we are dealing with particular distributions. In the example above, the raw data from two surveys are analysed without even taking into account the probability distribution. All that we are interested in is whether the two distributions are different.

To test with respect to a particular distribution, the procedure is exactly the same. For example, suppose that some time ago a restaurant conducted a survey which indicated the time a table remained occupied followed a normal distribution with mean 45 minutes and standard deviation 15 minutes. Its booking policy has been based on these figures. Recently problems have occurred and it is decided to check that these figures remain valid. A survey is conducted which gives the results shown in the first two columns of Table 11.3.

To calculate the expected values, the first thing which must be done is to standardize the class boundaries using the equation:

$$Z= \frac{x-\mu}{\sigma}$$

where μ is 45 and σ is 15. This procedure gives the Z-boundaries shown in column 3 of Table 11.3. We can use these boundaries to establish, using the standard normal probability tables, the proportion of values which would be found in each class if the distribution is normal with mean 45 and standard deviation 15.

Multiplying these probabilities (column 4 of Table 11.3) by the total frequency gives the expected value of each class (column 5). Once we have these values the x^2 test is performed precisely as before.

The calculated value of x^2 is 2.375. Testing at the 5% significance level with 6 degrees of freedom, the critical value of x^2 is 12.592. Hence in this case we can accept the null hypothesis, table occupation times are still normally distributed with mean 45 and standard deviation 15 minutes. The problems with the booking policy appear to be the result of bad luck and the problem should resolve itself without the need for a policy change.

Table 11.3　*Chi-squared test of goodness of fit to a normal distribution*

Time table occupied (minutes)	Observed values	Z-boundaries	Probabilities	Expected values
Under 20	8	Under −1.67	0.0475	8.36
20 to less than 30	21	−1.67 to <−1.00	0.1112	19.57
30 to less than 40	30	−1.00 to <−0.33	0.2120	37.31
40 to less than 50	45	−0.33 to < 0.33	0.2586	45.51
50 to less than 60	40	0.33 to < 1.00	0.2120	37.31
60 to less than 70	22	1.00 to < 1.67	0.1112	19.57
70 and over	10	1.67 and over	0.0475	8.36
Total frequency	176			

Contingency tests

The second area where the x^2 test is especially useful is in what are called contingency tests. Here we test whether two variables are independent of one another. The great advantage of the x^2 test is that as we are working with the observed frequencies we can use qualitative as well as quantitative variables. A qualitative variable is one which may be used to classify the data set but on which it is difficult or nonsensical to perform calculations. Many qualitative variables exist – the geographical location of guests, type of employment, political affiliation, college subject studied, etc. Given the importance of qualitative variables, it is extremely useful to have a test which enables the relationship between them to be investigated.

Suppose for instance that the company is examining its manager recruitment policy. On the basis of various performance criteria, it has classified its managers into a number of categories – exceptional, above-average, average, below-average. It wishes to see whether this classification is related to the educational achievement of the manager. The company has a number of different education indicators (degree or not, type of degree, grade of degree, etc). To begin with, it decides to test whether the kind of education is related to managerial performance. The results are presented in Table 11.4.

Table 11.4 *Managerial performance and education*

Education	Managerial Performance Exceptional O	E	Above-average O	E	Average O	E	Below-average O	E	Total
Hotel and catering degree or diploma	18	14.6	21	27.6	22	20.8	20	18.0	81
Other degree or diploma	9	8.1	12	15.3	10	11.6	14	10.0	45
No degree or diploma	25	29.3	65	55.1	42	41.6	30	36.0	162
Total	52		98		74		64		288

Table 11.4 is called a contingency table since all contingencies are included – each manager has to be classified somewhere in the table. We begin then with the observed values (0).

We then establish the null hypothesis. In this case, this is that there is no relationship between managerial performance and kind of education: i.e.

$$H_0 : \text{the two categories are independent}$$

This hypothesis is tested against the alternative that they are not independent: i.e.

$$H_1 : \text{the two categories are dependent}$$

If H_0 is true, then to find the expected values we can apply the multiplication rule of probability for independent events that was discussed in Chapter 4. This rule states that for two independent events (A and B) the probability of both occurring is given by the product of their individual probabilities: i.e.

$$P(A \cap B) = P(A) \times P(B)$$

In this case we consider each cell of the table in turn. Beginning with the first, there are 52 exceptional managers in the total of 288. Hence, if a manager is selected at random, the probability that he or she is rated exceptional is 52/288. Similarly, there are 81 managers with a hotel and catering qualification from a total of 288, and the probability that a manager chosen at random has such a qualification is therefore 81/288. The probability that he or she is exceptional and with a hotel and catering qualification is given by the product of the two (52/288 × 81/288 = 4212/82944 = 0.05078).

Since the probability of any one manager having these two characteristics is 0.05078, out of 288 managers we would expect to find 0.05078 × 288 = 14.625 having both characteristics.

Hence

$$E = P(A \cap B) \times GT = P(A) \times P(B) \times GT$$

where E is the expected value and GT the grand total (288 in this example). But we know that

$$P(A) = RT/GT \text{ and } P(B) = CT/GT$$

where RT is the row total and CT is the column total. Substituting we obtain:

$$E = RT/GT \times CT/GT \times GT$$

We can divide out two of the GTs, leaving the following equation for the calculation of the expected value of any cell:

$$E = (RT \times CT)/GT$$

This equation is often presented without explanation. However, we can see that it is not some magic formula but is derived directly from basic probability theory. Using this equation all of the expected values in Table 11.4 can be calculated. For example, the first cell is found as $(81 \times 52)/288 = 14.625$ as shown.

The calculation of the test value of x^2 now follows the same procedure as previously. For each cell we find the square of the difference between the observed and expected values, and then divide by the expected value. Note that all of the expected values are over 5 so there is no need to combine classes. The results for each cell are then summed to give the overall x^2 statistic.

In the case of the first cell we have $(18-14.6)^2/14.6 = 0.7918$; and the values for the other cells are found likewise. The calculated value of x^2 comes out as 8.643.

The critical value of x^2 depends again on the significance level of the test and the degrees of freedom. In this case, we are constraining the problem in the sense that the row and column totals have to be the same with the observed and expected values. We ensure that this constraint is met since we use these totals to calculate the expected values. This means that we have one constraint on the rows and one on the columns. The number of degrees of freedom will therefore be equal to the number of rows less one multiplied by the number of columns less one. That is:

$$\text{df} = (r-1) \times (c-1).$$

In this example, we have 4 rows and 3 columns, giving 6 degrees of freedom. If we test at the 5% significance level, we already know that the critical x^2 value is 12.592. Hence we accept H_o, the evidence available suggests that the managerial performance is unrelated to the kind of education followed. The company would therefore have to carry on looking for other factors on which to base its managerial selection policy.

The application of the x^2 test always follows the above steps. One point to note however concerns the situation where a 2×2 contingency table is used. This results in only one degree of freedom. It has been observed that x^2 is unreliable in this case and a simple correction called *Yates correction factor* should be applied. This is that we subtract 0.5 from the absolute difference of O−E prior to squaring. In other words the correction operates to reduce the size of the squared value whether O−E is positive or negative. The amended equation for the calculation of the x^2 test statistic in this case is:

$$x^2 = \Sigma \frac{(\,|\,O-E\,|\, - 0.5\,)^2}{E}$$

Note that there is some dispute between statisticians whether this correction is really useful. However, it seems worth applying in that, other things being equal, it reduces the chances of a type-I error. This error is probably the more important one for most business-type tests.

Having looked at the x^2 test, we now go on to look at a couple of other non-parametric tests to give an indication of the kind of test that is available.

The Wilcoxon rank-sum test

This is designed to test whether two samples come from the same population or from two different ones. As its name suggests the test works by considering only the rank (or position) of values in the two samples rather than the values themselves. Note that the test requires relatively large samples (10 minimum per sample). The samples do not however have to be of the same size. The logic of the test is best explained by an example.

A hotel is considering installing mini-bars in all bedrooms. It decides to investigate the effect that this has on the amount spent on drinks per customer-night by installing the bars in a limited number of rooms. It then compares the amount spent in rooms with the mini-bars compared to those where the guest must rely on room service. The results of the test are shown in Table 11.5.

Table 11.5   *Amount spent on drinks per guest-night*

Rooms with mini-bars	Rooms relying on room service
2.63	1.95
8.28	1.45
0.40	22.50
1.65	7.56
14.68	0
0	5.20
2.30	0
0	11.20
3.47	3.90
3.23	5.10

Note: The two samples have deliberately been kept as small as possible so as to avoid ending up with an enormous table whose only purpose is to show the principles underlying the calculations. In practice, the use of a statistical package such as SPSS facilitates calculations on large samples. Alternatively a spreadsheet may be used.

The test combines the two samples and re-writes the observations in order. The ranks of the amounts spent under each system are then examined. If there is a difference then we should find one set of rooms at one end of the table and the other set at the other end. For example, if rooms with mini-bars always sold more drinks then they would always rank higher than rooms without. In such a case, the conclusion would easily be reached that mini-bars were worth having. Unfortunately, situations are rarely clear-cut in this kind of way. It is where there is a mixture of ranks that the Wilcoxon rank-sum test can help.

If the calculations are being done by hand, then the easiest method is to construct a table such as Table 11.6.

Table 11.6 makes it easy to see the ranks of the observations in each sample. These ranks are then summed, giving the test its name. Note that if two or more observations are ranked equally, as is the case with zero here, then the ranks that they should have occupied are averaged (i.e. 1+2+3+4 divided by 4 which gives 2.5).

Table 11.6 *Amount spent on drinks per guest night*

Mini-bars	Room service	Ranks sample 1	Ranks sample 2
0		2.5	
0		2.5	
	0		2.5
	0		2.5
0.40		5	
	1.45		6
1.65		7	
	1.95		8
2.30		9	
2.63		10	
3.23		11	
3.47		12	
	3.90		13
	5.10		14
	5.20		15
	7.56		16
8.28		17	
	11.20		18
14.68		19	
	22.50		20
		Σ 95	Σ 115

Once the rank-sums have been calculated, one of them is chosen as the test statistic. As we will see presently, it does not matter which one.

The hypothesis to be tested is that the two samples come from the same population – that is, in this case, the amount spent on drinks is the same whether the room has a mini-bar or room service. Hence:

$$H_0 : \text{samples identical}$$
$$H_1 : \text{samples not identical}$$

The above test has been set up as a two-tailed test. Conceivably it would be more logical to test whether the amount spent is greater with mini-bars since this is the decision of interest to the hotel management. We will consider this test in a moment.

If H_0 is true, then the sum of the ranks should be equal to their mean value. That is, the ranks of the two samples should be evenly spread. Assuming that sample 1 has been chosen as the test statistic, this mean is calculated as:

$$\mu= \frac{n_1 (n_1 + n_2 + 1)}{2} \qquad (11.2)$$

In the above example, this mean is evaluated as:

$$\mu= \frac{10 (10+10+1)}{2} =105$$

Note that because the samples are of equal size, this is just half the sum of the ranks.

As usual, however, we cannot simply compare the expected mean with the value found from the two samples because of the problem of sampling variability. The variance must also be taken into account. Wilcoxon showed that the variance of the rank-sum (σ^2) is given by the following equation:

$$\sigma^2= \frac{(n_1 \times n_2) \times (n_1 + n_2 + 1)}{12} \qquad (11.3)$$

In this case we have:

$$\sigma^2= \frac{(10 \times 10) \times (10 + 10 + 1)}{12} =175$$

The standard deviation is then found in the usual way by square rooting the variance:

$$\sigma= \sqrt{\sigma^2} =13.23$$

Wilcoxon showed, moreover, that provided neither sample was smaller than 10 (note again that the two samples do NOT have to be the same size), the rank-sum was approximately normally distributed.

The hypothesis test follows classic lines from this point. We standardize the calculated rank-sum (denoted as W) via the usual equation:

$$Z= \frac{W-\mu}{\sigma} = \frac{95-105}{13.23} =0.756$$

A significance level is then assigned to the test so that the critical

Z-values may be determined. Setting the significance level at 5% gives critical values of $+1.96$ and -1.96 (since this is a two-tailed test).

The calculated Z-value is then compared to the critical values in the usual way. Here we can see that the calculated value lies in the acceptance region and we therefore accept H_o, the average spend per night does not seem to differ between rooms with and without mini-bars. Further investment in such bars would appear to be of doubtful value.

If the rank-sum of sample 2 had been taken as the test statistic this would have made no difference to the conclusion, since the standardized value would have been -0.756 (as the reader might like to verify).

A one-tailed test is easily established. We merely write, for example:

H_o : average spend identical
H_1 : average spend greater with mini-bars

The critical Z-value changes (for the given 5% significance level) to 1.645. H_o would still therefore be accepted.

The Spearman rank-correlation test

The Wilcoxon test looks at whether two samples come from different populations. The Spearman rank-correlation test looks at whether two variables are related to one another. Where numerical data are available, more powerful methods exist for the analysis of correlation. These methods are considered in the next chapter. Spearman's test is particularly useful for testing data sets where only ranks are available.

For example, suppose the trade union official at a hotel is trying to persuade management that the hotel is understaffed during times of high occupancy. To test this claim, it is decided to compare complaints from guests regarding service with occupancy level. Over a year, 10 days are chosen at random and ranked according to complaints and occupancy. The results are given in Table 11.7.

From this basic data, we calculate the Spearman rank-correlation coefficient. This coefficient, which we will denote as S, is given as:

$$S = 1 - \frac{6 \times \Sigma d^2}{n(n^2 - 1)} \qquad (11.4)$$

The variable S can take on values from plus to minus one. A value of plus one indicates a perfect positive relationship between the ranks; minus one, a perfect negative relationship. A value of zero means there is no relationship.

Table 11.7   *Complaints and occupancy: a Spearman rank correlation test*

Day	Occupancy rank	Complaints rank	Difference	Squared difference
1	5	7	−2	4
2	1	3	−2	4
3	8	8	0	0
4	10	6	4	16
5	4	5	−1	1
6	2	1	1	1
7	9	10	−1	1
8	6	9	−3	9
9	3	2	1	1
10	7	4	3	9
				Σ 46

Applying Equation 11.4 to the data in Table 11.7 gives:

$$S = 1 - \frac{6 \times 46}{10\,(100 - 1)} = 0.72$$

This value indicates that there is a reasonable positive relationship between the two ranks, appearing to support the union case. We can however conduct a hypothesis test to check whether the value found is statistically significant.

We conduct a hypothesis in the usual style where we test:

$$H_o : \mu_s = 0$$
$$H_1 : \mu_s > 0$$

If there is no relationship between the two variables then we know that S will equal zero so the null hypothesis is equivalent to testing that the two rankings are independent.

Provided that the sample size is at least 10, if there is no correlation, S is normally distributed with mean 0 and variance $1/(n-1)$. We can therefore standardize our calculated S using the usual equation:

$$Z = \frac{S - \mu_s}{\sigma_s} = \frac{0.72 - 0}{\sqrt{(1 / 10 - 1)}} = 2.16$$

The critical Z-value for a 5% level of significance (one-tailed test) is 1.65. Hence we reject H_o; the correlation is significantly different from zero and is not due to chance factors.

Conclusion

In this chapter we have looked at non-parametric methods of hypothesis testing. These methods are extremely useful because they allow tests to be undertaken in situations where the calculation of summary measures make no sense. One difficulty with the measures is that as they work with the data set rather than a summary measure they may involve a lot of arithmetic. The use of a computer is strongly recommended when using these tests. Most of the calculations are easily and quickly accomplished using a spreadsheet. Alternatively, a dedicated statistical package such as SPSS might be used.

Further reading

CONOVER, W. (1980), *Practical Nonparametric Statistics* (Wiley, Chichester, 2nd edition).
DANIEL, W. (1978), *Applied Nonparametric Statistics* (Houghton Mifflin, London).
SIEGEL, S. and CASTELLAN, J. jnr (1988), *Nonparametric Statistics for the Behavioural Sciences* (McGraw-Hill, London, 2nd edition).

Exercises

1   A restaurant chain wishes to assess the quality of service provided by its restaurants. A pilot study is introduced to two restaurants whereby customers are invited to mark confidentially the service out of 100. The results are:

Marks	*Restaurant* 1	*Restaurant* 2
0 to < 20	15	18
20 to < 40	22	20
40 to < 60	32	35
60 to < 80	41	36
80 to <100	20	14

(a) Use the x^2 test to determine whether, at the 5% level, there is a significant difference in the standard of service provided by the two restaurants.

(b) Conduct the same test as a difference between two means.

(c) Compare the results of the two tests. Would it make a difference if the class widths were not all the same?

2   The following table shows the average monthly salary levels (calculated on a consistent basis) and star ratings of hotels. Test the hypothesis that the two are independent.

Hotel rating Monthly salary	*****	****	***	**	*
less than 1000	51	120	148	200	140
1000 to <1500	85	185	210	230	112
1500 to <2000	90	162	165	154	98
2000 to <2500	45	74	85	90	60
2500 to <3000	21	35	30	38	23
3000 and over	8	12	10	2	1

3   At present, a hotel asks all people who book by telephone to confirm their booking in writing. The hotel manager finds the system cumbersome to operate and does not feel it makes much difference to the number of no-shows. However, he does not wish to abandon the system if it is working.

Over a survey period, he finds that of the people who *confirmed in writing* their telephone booking 6,080 appeared and 920 did not; whilst of those who *did not confirm* 2,562 turned up and 438 did not.

At what level is the difference between confirmed and unconfirmed reservations statistically significant?

On the basis of your calculations, would you advise the manager to keep or abandon the system?

4   A hotel manager contends that occupancy is unrelated to season. Hotel records kept over a thirty year period reveal the following average occupancies per season. What is to be concluded about the manager's contention?

	Winter	Spring	Summer	Autumn
OCCUPANCY				
less than 30%	13	12	7	12
30% to <60%	10	9	12	10
over 60%	7	9	11	8

5   Union officials complain that hours worked per week have increased over a 2-year period due to understaffing. Payroll records of 20 workers are drawn at random for the current month and the same month 2 years ago. The data are as follows. Do they support the union case?

Hours per week

2 years ago	50	51	43	44	41	50	43	54	41	65	45	43	45	66	37	48	52	59	38	44
Now	44	58	56	40	55	43	48	50	39	38	55	60	53	42	54	61	49	43	56	59

6 Ten hotels are ranked according to price and occupancy. Do the data indicate a correlation between the two variables?

Hotel	A	B	C	D	E	F	G	H	I	J
Price	8	2	3	10	4	1	7	5	6	9
Occupancy	4	6	7	5	1	8	9	2	10	3

12
The analysis of time-series data

In business, data sets are often of a time-series nature, that is we have observations of a particular variable over time on, for example, a monthly or an annual basis. This chapter considers some of the many methods that might be used to present and particularly to analyse this kind of data set.

One common method of presentation is the use of index numbers (which we touched upon in Chapter 2). Most people are familiar, for instance, with the retail price index. We begin the chapter by looking at how such indexes may be constructed.

Where we have two or more sets of data, we are often interested to discover whether there is a relationship between them. The techniques of correlation and regression are particularly useful in this context and the chapter considers these next.

Finally, it is frequently useful to try to project time series into the future. A variety of forecasting methods exist and we close the chapter by discussing some of these.

Index numbers

The idea of an index number is to indicate the change in, say, prices over a particular time period. Although the best known example is probably the retail price index, many other common examples exist, for instance, the exchange-rate index and the stock exchange index. Using these index numbers it is possible (provided that the series of numbers is meaningfully constructed) to say that, for example, 'prices' were $x\%$ higher in 1990 than in 1980. In this section, we shall briefly review the way in which index numbers are constructed. We will use the example of a price index.

The easiest way of constructing index numbers is to use the simple aggregate method. Here we just sum the prices of items in the current year and express them as a percentage of the base year. Although this technique is simple to apply, it fails to take into account the relative importance of the various components of the index. For this reason, weighted index numbers are generally preferred.

Each item in the index is given a weight to reflect its importance. This importance is purely a subjective matter, as is the choice of items to include in the index. The general determination of the index numbers then follows one of two methods – the relative or the aggregative.

The relative method takes the price of each item in the current year (n) and divides by its price in the base year (b), and multiplies by 100 to give a result in index number form. This result is then multiplied by the item's weight in the index. This procedure is repeated for all items in the index and the results are summed. The value of the index is then found by dividing by the sum of the weights. This method is summarized by Equation 12.1.

$$\text{Relative price index} = \{ \Sigma [((p_n/p_b) \times 100) \times w] \} / \Sigma w \quad (12.1)$$

The aggregate method takes the price of each item in the base year, multiplies by its weight and sums the results. This exercise is then repeated for the current year. The current year sum is then expressed as a percentage of the base year to give the value of the index. This method is summarized by Equation 12.2:

$$\text{Aggregate price index} = \frac{\Sigma (p_n \times w)}{\Sigma (p_b \times w)} \times 100 \quad (12.2)$$

In both cases it is usual to multiply the result by 100 to express the index number as a percentage. To see these two methods in operation suppose that we have the information in Table 12.1.

Applying Equations (12.1) and (12.2) to the data contained in Table 12.1, we can see how the different methods treat inflation. Looking first at the relative method, we have:

Relative index for year n = 3318.9/28 = 118.53%

The aggregate method gives:

Aggregate index for year n = 3126/2473 = 1.2641 = 126.41%

In other words, prices were 18% or 26% higher in year n than they were in year b, depending on the method used and taking into account the relative importance of the different items included in the index.

Table 12.1   *Price data for typical student diet*

Item	W	p_b	p_n	(p_n/p_b) $\times 100$	$(p_n/p_b \times 100)$ $\times w$	$p_b \times w$	$p_n \times w$
Bread	10	46	52	113.0	1130.0	460	520
Wine	4	152	156	102.6	410.4	608	624
Paté de foie gras	1	1053	1542	146.4	146.4	1053	1542
Tea	5	24	32	133.3	666.5	120	160
Baked Beans	8	29	35	120.7	965.6	232	280
	$\Sigma 28$				$\Sigma 3318.9$	$\Sigma 2473$	$\Sigma 3126$

An important feature of the index is the precise way that the weights are calculated. In the above example, they have been chosen at random. In practice, however, they would represent the quantities consumed on average by those for whom the index is constructed. If the index is the retail price index of the country then a study will be undertaken of the quantities typically consumed of different items and these quantities will be used as weights.

A number of quantity-weighted price indices exist. First, there is the *Laspeyre price index*. Here quantities consumed in the base year are used as the weights. In other words, a typical household bill is calculated for the base year and the cost of purchasing the same quantities of the same items is calculated for the current year. This gives the following equations for the calculation of index numbers using the relative and aggregate method.

$$\text{Laspeyre relative price index year n} = \frac{\Sigma \left[((p_n/p_b) \times 100) \times p_b q_b \right]}{\Sigma p_b q_b}$$

$$\text{Laspeyre aggregate price index year n} = \frac{\Sigma (p_n \times q_b)}{\Sigma (p_b \times q_b)} \times 100$$

An alternative approach is the *Paasche price index*. In this case, the quantities consumed in the current year are used as weights so that the index number relates the cost of purchasing the amounts currently being purchased with what it would have cost to purchase these amounts in the base year. This gives the equation:

Paasche relative price index year n=
$$\frac{\Sigma \; [((p_n/p_b)\times 100)\times p_n q_n]}{\Sigma p_n q_n}$$

Paasche aggregate price index year n=
$$\frac{\Sigma \; (p_n \times q_b)}{\Sigma \; (p_n \times q_n)} \times 100$$

The Laspeyre index provides a better indication of pure price inflation. The Paasche index includes price inflation but also the response of consumers to different price changes in different goods. The Paasche index is better as a cost-of-living index since it reflects what consumers are now paying compared to what they would have had to pay for the same items. In a way both indices are required – one to indicate how prices have changed over a period and the other to indicate what the impact of these price changes has been, once allowance has been made for changes in consumption patterns.

In practice however the Laspeyre index is far more widely used. There are two main reasons for this. First, since the Paasche uses current year quantity weights, these weights must be re-estimated each year. This may involve terrific expense. Second, in the Laspeyre index, the denominator stays constant so that it is possible to compare the current year with other years in the series. In the Paasche, the denominator changes each year so that the current year can only be compared to the base.

A crucial issue with both indexes, but especially the Laspeyre, is the choice of base year. In particular there is the problem of when to update the base. This becomes increasingly necessary with the Laspeyre as time passes since there tends to be more and more difference between the quantity weights and the current year quantities. Unfortunately the choice of base is something of a political football. By choosing the base year carefully, it is possible to improve the look of the series, at least for a while. For instance, in the case of retail prices, if a month is chosen when inflation was abnormally high, the index for other months will be depressed.

Linear correlation and regression

When we have two or more sets of data, it is often of interest to see if and how they are related to one another. The techniques of correlation and regression are two (amongst many) methods that allow such relationships to be estimated. Correlation indicates the *degree* to which the variables are related. Regression indicates *how* they are related. In this section we shall examine the case of two variables that are thought to be related linearly.

Linear correlation

Suppose that hotel management wishes to test the extent to which occupancy is related to price. A random sample of 10 nights is taken from hotel records. The average price is calculated for rooms sold that night and is compared with the occupancy level. The resulting data set is presented in Table 12.1. Given this data, to what extent is the occupancy rate related to the price charged?

Before using correlation analysis to provide a numerical answer, it is always worthwhile looking at a *scatter diagram* of the data set – that is, a graph showing the location of each of the data points (night 1, night 2, etc.). The scatter diagram of the data in Table 12.2 is presented in Figure 12.1.

From Figure 12.1 it is clear that there is no precise relationship between occupancy and price – that is, knowing one does not allow us to predict the other precisely. Nonetheless, there appears to be an inverse relationship between the variables, high prices are associated with low occupancy and

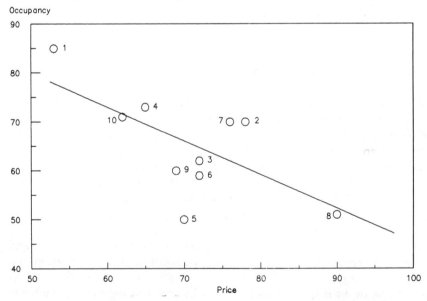

Figure 12.1 *Hotel occupancy and price scatter diagram and regression line*

Table 12.2 *Average price per room sold and occupancy*

Night	Price	Occupancy
1	53	85
2	78	70
3	72	62
4	65	73
5	70	50
6	72	59
7	76	70
8	90	51
9	69	60
10	62	71

vice versa. It is important to note that such an association says nothing about causation – low occupancy may be due to high prices, but equally high prices may be due to low occupancy. It will depend on the pricing policy of the hotel. Clearly, the policy implications of the relationship between the two variables is not the same in the two cases and so the issue of causation must always be carefully considered.

Given that there appears to be some inverse relationship between the two variables, we will now consider how to express the strength of the association numerically. An index of the strength of a linear relationship is provided by the sample correlation coefficient.

The sample correlation coefficient

When we considered a single data set, we described its variability in terms of deviations from the mean, $x - \bar{x}$ (see Chapter 3). Now that each data point is determined by two variables, we can describe its variability with reference to its deviation from both means, $x - \bar{x}$ and $y - \bar{y}$. The difficulty is how to combine these two measures into one.

An obvious approach would be to add them. Unfortunately, this method would give misleading answers. Suppose for example that the y value never changed. In this case any variation that there is in the data comes entirely from x. There is no *co-variation* – that is, the two variables do not move together. If we add the two elements however we will give the impression that there is some co-variation. What is required therefore is a measure that will be zero if *either* of the two elements is zero. The easiest way to accomplish this is to multiply the two parts together and this is what is done in statistics.

For each data point the co-variation is given as:

$$\text{cov}(x,y) = (x-\bar{x}) \times (y-\bar{y})$$

and we then sum these values over the data set giving:

$$\text{total co-variation} = \Sigma\text{cov}(x,y) = \Sigma\,[\,(x-\bar{x}) \times (y-\bar{y})\,]$$

This is the basic equation used to measure correlation. It suffers, however, two drawbacks. First, its value will depend on the number of data points. As we add observations to the data set the total co-variation will carry on increasing even if the new points are closer to the means than previous ones. This problem is avoided in the usual manner by dividing the total co-variation by the number of data points (n). Second, the total co-variation will depend on the specific location of the data set (i.e. whether the values are basically 'high' or 'low'). To avoid this problem the measure is standardized (exactly as with the Z-value, for example) by dividing by the standard deviation. Since the data set is variable with respect to x *and* y, we must divide by both standard deviations. This gives the standardized sample correlation coefficient (denoted by r):

$$r = \frac{\Sigma\ (x-\bar{x}) \times (y-\bar{y})}{n \times s_x \times s_y} \tag{12.3}$$

Any computer-based statistics package that includes regression will calculate the value of r. In addition, many spreadsheet and integrated packages produce r as a routine value. Alternatively, a spreadsheet may be used simply to calculate the various totals. In this case (and where a computer is not available) it is more efficient to expand Equation (12.3), which should be considered the *definition* of r, into Equation (12.4), which may be used as a *computational equation* for r.

$$r = \frac{(n \times \Sigma xy) - (\Sigma x \times \Sigma y)}{\sqrt{\{\,[(n \times \Sigma x^2) - (\Sigma x)^2] \times [(n \times \Sigma y^2) - (\Sigma y)^2]\,\}}} \tag{12.4}$$

Despite its more formidable appearance, Equation (12.4) greatly simplifies calculation, especially when new values are added to the data set. It is similar in this respect to the computational formula for the variance introduced in Chapter 3.

Applying Equation (12.4) to the data in Table 12.2 results in Table 12.3.

Table 12.3 *Calculation of the sample correlation coefficient*

Night	Price (x)	Occupancy (y)	x^2	y^2	xy
1	53	85	2809	7225	4505
2	78	70	6084	4900	5460
3	72	62	5184	3844	4464
4	65	73	4225	5329	4745
5	70	50	4900	2500	3500
6	72	59	5184	3481	4248
7	76	70	5776	4900	5320
8	90	51	8100	2601	4590
9	69	60	4761	3600	4140
10	62	71	3844	5041	4402
	Σ 707	Σ 651	Σ 50867	Σ 43421	Σ 45374

Substituting the values calculated in Table 12.3 into Equation (12.4) gives

$$r = \frac{(10 \times 45374) - (707 \times 651)}{\sqrt{[(10 \times 50867 - 707^2) \times (10 \times 43421 - 651^2)]}} = 0.680118$$

Having calculated r, we must interpret what it means. Two things are of importance – the sign and the value. First, note that the sign is negative indicating an inverse relationship between occupancy and price. Second, since r is a standardized measure its value cannot exceed one. As one would expect a value of one indicates an exact relationship between two variables. In this case, the value found indicates that there is some relationship between the variables but this is some way from being exact. A value of zero indicates that there is no linear relationship between the variables. In such a case, care must always be taken that there is not a non-linear relationship. The easiest way to check for this is simply to plot the data set on a scatter diagram. Figure 12.2 gives some examples of data sets with their r-values.

The limitation of the technique that the relationship must be linear is not as restrictive as it might at first appear since it is often possible to transform variables so that a linear relationship emerges. For example the relationship, $y = 0.5 \times x^2$ is non-linear. However, if we define a new variable z, where $z = x^2$ then substituting, $y = 0.5z$, which is linear. We can then work with the linear form and transform back to the original units at the end of the analysis. This technique is applied in the later section on forecasting.

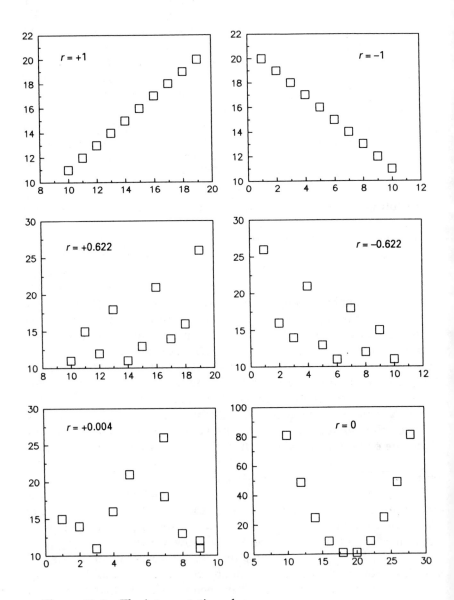

Figure 12.2   *The interpretation of* r

Linear regression

Correlation tells us the strength of the relationship between two variables. Regression shows the way in which they are related. To apply regression one variable must be designated as the dependent one. This designation must be done on sound theoretical grounds. In this case we will test the standard economic theory that occupancy depends on price.

The idea underlying regression is simple. We are trying to find the straight line that gives the best approximation of the relationship between occupancy and price. Once we have identified this line, we can use it to predict occupancy for different prices. Depending on the spread of values around the line, such predictions will be more or less accurate.

One way of identifying the line would simply be to draw it freehand onto the scatter diagram. Interestingly, as is clear from Figure 12.2, this method will work well if the relationship between the two variables is strong. At the limit, if $r=\pm1$ then you would merely have to join up the points. However, as the data set spreads out it becomes increasingly open to interpretation where to position the line. More to the point, however, is the fact that drawing the line can only work in the two variable case. If we add more independent variables, a mathematical approach has to be adopted.

The method used to position the line works via the errors (or residuals). If r is anything other than ±1, then whatever line is drawn through the data set will involve an error. This error is measured by the difference between the value of the dependent variable predicted by the line (denoted as y_p) and the true value, y. The line chosen is then the one that minimizes the total of these errors taking into account all data points. Note that simply adding up the errors does not work because once again we run into the problem that the sum is zero. And once again the solution is adopted of squaring the errors before summing them. The chosen line is then the one that gives the smallest sum of squared errors and for this reason it is called the least squares regression line.

Formally then we are trying to find the values of a and b in the following equation:

$$y_p = a + bx$$

such that

$$\Sigma e^2 \text{ is minimized, where } e = y - y_p$$

As with r, many computer-based packages include routines that calculate the values of a and b. If you do not have access to such a package, the following equations may be used to calculate b and a.

$$b= \frac{(n \times \Sigma xy) - (\Sigma x \times \Sigma y)}{(n \times \Sigma x^2) - (\Sigma x)^2} \qquad (12.5)$$

$$a= \quad \bar{y} - b\bar{x} = \Sigma y/n - b\Sigma x/n \qquad (12.6)$$

Note that if the value of r has already been calculated, then all of the values needed for b and a will already have been calculated. Substituting the appropriate values into these equations gives:

$$b= \frac{(10 \times 45374) - (707 \times 651)}{(10 \times 50867 - 707^2)} = -0.73881$$

$$a= \quad 651/10 - (-0.73881) \times (707/10) \qquad = 117.334$$

Hence the least squares regression line is:

$$y_p = 117.334 - 0.73881x$$

This line is shown in Figure 12.1. As can be seen it approximates the data set reasonably well. Unfortunately, 'reasonably well' is not really adequate as a description of how well the estimated line fits the data set and so quantitative methods have been devised to test this. A number of approaches suggest themselves.

A common approach is to calculate r^2 (i.e. the sample correlation coefficient squared). This is called the *coefficient of determination*. In the example above, r^2 is $0.680118^2 = 0.46256$. As we can see the calculation of r^2 is simple, but what does it tell us? Suppose for a moment that we had no knowledge of the relationship between y and x. If asked to predict y, the best that we can do is take the mean value, $\bar{y}$. The error that we make will then depend on the difference between the true value and the mean value, that is $y-\bar{y}$. Once we know the regression line, then we can predict y (y_p) on the basis of x. The error that we make is now the difference between the true value and the predicted value, that is $y-y_p$. This error is said to be *unexplained* by the regression line. The better the regression line fits the data sets, the smaller will be the unexplained error. If $r=\pm1$, then the regression line will follow the observed points exactly and there will be no unexplained error. All of the error with respect to the mean will therefore have been *explained*. The coefficient of determination (r^2) measures the proportion of the squared error that has been explained.

A second approach is to consider the values of a and b individually, especially b. The estimates that we have for these values come from a sample. As always there is a possibility that the relationship observed in the sample is due to chance and that there is no real relationship. To test this we can conduct a hypothesis test along the lines of Chapters 8 and 9. If there is no real relationship then the population value of b (β) will be zero. We adopt this as our null hypothesis and test against the alternative that β is not zero. That is:

$$H_0 : \beta = 0$$
$$H_1 : \beta <> 0$$

The calculation of the test statistic follows the same general principles as previously although the calculation of the standard deviation of values around the slope (called the standard error of b) is a little complicated due to the fact that it depends on the variability of both y and x. The calculation of the test statistic is given by:

$$t = \frac{b - \beta}{\sqrt{[\Sigma(y - y_p)^2/n - 2 \; / \; (\Sigma x^2 \; - \; (\Sigma x)^2/n) \;]}} \qquad (12.7)$$

This value can be calculated using this equation. The values of y_p must be calculated for each data point using the regression line. The calculations are best done using a spreadsheet. Doing so and substituting the results into Equation (12.7) gives a calculated t-value of -2.62402. Generally, however, the t-value is taken directly from a computer-based regression package. Some packages just give t, some just give the standard error (i.e. the denominator of equation 12.7), others give both.

Once the test statistic is available, it is compared to a critical t-value in the usual way. In this case there are $n-2$ degrees of freedom. Taking a 5% significance level this gives critical (two-tailed) t-values of ± 2.306. Hence in this case we can reject the null hypothesis, the true value of β does not seem to be zero. The slope of the regression line is not just due to chance factors.

A hypothesis test can also be conducted on the intercept. Generally this is of much less interest since the point where the line crosses the Y-axis is usually a long way removed from the data set. Thus a regression line which has a significant constant but insignificant slope is useless, whereas one which has a significant slope is of interest regardless of the constant.

A final method of looking at the accuracy of the regression line is to use it to forecast values different to the ones that were used in its construction. Suppose for example that we have monthly data over a 5-year period. The standard approach is to use the first four years' data to estimate the equation and then use the final year to check how accurate are the predictions of the estimated equation.

It is to the issue of forecasting time-series data that we now turn.

Forecasting time series: decomposition methods

Having looked at the basic ideas of correlation and regression, it is possible to consider the analysis of time-series data. One approach to this analysis is to break the data set into its component parts. It is argued that any set of time-series data can be broken into four parts. These are:

1   A trend (*T*) showing long-term change.
2   A seasonal element (*S*) showing movement around the trend on an annual basis.
3   A cyclical element (*C*) showing movement around the trend over a number of years.
4   A residual element (*R*) showing random movement around the trend.

If these four parts are put together then the original data set (*D*) is obtained.

The relationship between *D* and its four constituent parts may have one of two principal forms – either additive or multiplicative. That is, either

$$D=T+S+C+R$$

or

$$D=T\times S\times C\times R$$

The additive model assumes that the values of the seasonal and cyclical elements remain the same over the period being covered. This assumption will usually hold if the trend is not too marked. Where, however, the data set shows a clear upward or downward trend, a multiplicative model will generally give better results since only the proportions are assumed to remain the same. This difference will become clearer as we work through some examples.

The equations above define a general model. Not all elements need to be included every time. Indeed, the model that it is possible to construct will depend in part on the data available – for example, if annual data are all that is available, then it will not be possible to identify a seasonal element. Similarly, if the data set is over a relatively short period (say, less than 10 years) it will be difficult to identify a cyclical element.

With most data sets of relevance to the hotel and catering industry, it is the cyclical element that must be dropped.

An additive model

The easiest way to see how this model works is to consider an example. The data in Table 12.4 relate to percentage hotel bed occupancy in England over the period June 1971 to May 1975.

Table 12.4 *Hotel occupancy in England (June 1971–May 1975)*

Month Year	J	F	M	A	M	J	J	A	S	O	N	D
1971						60	65	67	63	50	35	30
1972	29	30	36	44	51	59	65	66	65	50	36	30
1973	31	34	38	44	49	56	64	67	63	50	37	30
1974	29	32	38	46	49	57	66	72	66	49	36	30
1975	29	33	39	39	49							

Source: English Tourist Board, Hotel Occupancy Surveys 1971–5 (presented in Medlik and Airey as part of Table 76)

The data in Table 12.4 are monthly so that it will be possible to identify the seasonal element. Not enough data exist, however, for a cycle to emerge and this part of the model will be dropped. Casual inspection of the data set reveals that it is quite stable with little obvious time trend so that an additive model should suffice. The data will therefore be analysed using the model:

$$D=T+S+R$$

The first thing that must be done then is to estimate the trend. A number of methods exist for this. One common approach is to use a moving average based on a certain number of periods. For example, we might decide to use a 5-month moving average. The trend value for August 1971 would then be found as (June 71 + July 71 + August 71 + September 71 + October 71)/5 – i.e. $(60+65+67+63+50)/5 = 61$. For September 1971, the trend value would be: $(65+67+63+50+35)/5 = 56$. In general, we take the value for the month itself plus the two months either side of it.

The moving average method is quite straightforward to apply, if rather long-winded. It suffers, however, a couple of drawbacks. First, with a 5-month moving average we lose 4 data points – two at the beginning and two at the end of the set because there is not enough data to calculate moving averages for these points. Second, and far more serious, it is impossible using the moving average method to derive forecasts for future years. In general, the use of methods (such as regression) that allow the projection of the trend into the future is to be preferred.

We saw in the previous section how to apply regression methods and we will use them here to estimate a trend line. In this example, we label the months from 1 (which is June 1971) to 48 (May 1975). We then regress occupancy against these time values to derive a trend line, which indicates to what extent occupancy is a function of time. Note, however, that the data set begins in June 1971 and ends in May 1975. If the complete data set is used to estimate the regression line, the results will be biased because we begin with high occupancy values for the first year and end with low occupancies of the final year. A negative bias will therefore be imparted to the calculated regression line. The results obtained confirm this problem. The regression line calculated using the complete data set is found (using SPSS) as follows (the values in brackets are the *t*-values):

$$T= \quad 50.66489 \quad - \quad 0.15214 \quad \times MONTH$$
$$\qquad (12.492) \qquad (1.056) \qquad\qquad\qquad r^2=0.02366$$

If, however, only the complete years (1972–4 i.e. quarters 8 to 43) are used, the estimated regression line becomes:

$$T= \quad 43.46521 \quad + \quad 0.1408 \quad \times MONTH$$
$$\qquad (7.013) \qquad (0.625) \qquad\qquad\qquad r^2=0.01138$$

The slope of the estimated trend line changes with the data used. The second equation seems more soundly based and will be used in the time-series analysis that follows. Note, however, that in both cases, the standard error of the slope confirms the casual impression that there is no time trend in the data set.

Once a trend equation has been calculated we can derive a de-trended series – that is, one where the variations are due only to S and R. For each month, we calculate a value for T from the above equation and we then subtract this value from D. Thus we have:

$$D-T=S+R$$

where $S+R$ is the de-trended series. This series is presented in Table 12.5.

The de-trended series is then used to separate the seasonal and residual elements. For each month of the year we have three values. We take the arithmetic mean of these three values for each month. This mean is calculated as $(\Sigma(D-T))/3$.

These mean values are the seasonal factors. As is apparent from the figures, there is a marked seasonal pattern with occupancy rising in the summer and falling in the winter. Theoretically, the trend line should pass through the 'centre' of the data set so that there are as many data points above the line as below. If we sum the seasonal factors across the year, then the result should be zero if this theoretical constraint has been met. In this case, the sum is 0.1, which seems close enough to zero, given the rounding of values that has already occurred (for instance, in the case of the trend values). In cases where the error is serious, a correction may be applied by dividing the error by the number of seasons (12 months, 4 quarters, 52 weeks, etc.). If the error is positive, the result is subtracted

Table 12.5   *The calculation of seasonal factors in an additive model*

1972	J	F	M	A	M	J	J	A	S	O	N	D
D	29	30	36	44	51	59	65	66	65	50	36	30
T	44.6	44.7	44.9	45.0	45.2	45.3	45.4	45.6	45.7	45.9	46.0	46.1
D−T	−15.6	−14.7	−8.9	−1.0	5.8	13.7	19.6	20.4	19.3	4.1	−10.0	−16.1
1973												
D	31	34	38	44	49	56	64	67	63	50	37	30
T	46.3	46.4	46.6	46.7	46.8	47.0	47.1	47.3	47.4	47.5	47.7	47.8
D−T	−15.3	−12.4	−8.6	−2.7	2.2	9.0	16.9	19.7	15.6	2.5	−10.7	−17.8
1974												
D	29	32	38	46	49	57	66	72	66	49	36	30
T	48.0	48.1	48.3	48.4	48.5	48.7	48.8	49.0	49.1	49.2	49.4	49.5
D−T	−19.0	−16.1	−10.3	−2.4	0.5	8.3	17.2	23.0	16.9	−0.2	−13.4	−19.5
$\dfrac{\Sigma\,(D-T)}{3}$	−16.6	−14.4	−9.2	−2.0	2.8	10.3	17.9	21.1	17.3	2.1	−11.4	−17.8

Table 12.6   *The calculation of residuals and forecast values in an additive seasonal model*

1971	J	F	M	A	M	J	J	A	S	O	N	D
D						60	65	67	63	50	35	30
T						43.6	43.7	43.9	44.0	44.2	44.3	44.5
S						10.3	17.9	21.1	17.3	2.1	-11.4	-17.8
F						54.0	61.6	65.0	61.3	46.3	33.0	26.6
FE						6.0	3.4	2.0	1.7	3.7	2.0	3.4
1972												
D	29	30	36	44	51	59	65	66	65	50	36	30
T	44.6	44.7	44.9	45.0	45.2	45.3	45.4	45.6	45.7	45.9	46.0	46.1
D–T	-15.6	-14.7	- 8.9	- 1.0	5.8	13.7	19.6	20.4	19.3	4.1	-10.0	-16.1
S	-16.6	-14.4	- 9.2	- 2.0	2.8	10.3	17.9	21.1	17.3	2.1	-11.4	-17.8
R	1.0	- 0.3	0.4	1.0	3.0	3.4	1.7	- 0.6	2.0	2.0	1.4	1.7
1973												
D	31	34	38	44	49	56	64	67	63	50	37	30
T	46.3	46.4	46.6	46.7	46.8	47.0	47.1	47.3	47.4	47.5	47.7	47.8
D–T	-15.3	-12.4	- 8.6	- 2.7	2.2	9.0	16.9	19.7	15.6	2.5	-10.7	-17.8
S	-16.6	-14.4	- 9.2	- 2.0	2.8	10.3	17.9	21.1	17.3	2.1	-11.4	-17.8
R	1.3	2.0	0.7	- 0.7	- 0.7	- 1.3	- 1.0	- 1.3	- 1.7	0.3	0.7	- 0.0

1974

D	29	32	38	46	49	57	66	72	66	49	36	30
T	48.0	48.1	48.3	48.4	48.5	48.7	48.8	49.0	49.1	49.2	49.4	49.5
D–T	−19.0	−16.1	−10.3	− 2.4	0.5	8.3	17.2	23.0	16.9	− 0.2	−13.4	−19.5
S	−16.6	−14.4	− 9.2	− 2.0	2.8	10.3	17.9	21.1	17.3	2.1	−11.4	−17.8
R	− 2.4	− 1.7	− 1.0	− 0.4	− 2.4	− 2.0	− 0.7	2.0	− 0.4	− 2.4	− 2.0	− 1.7

1975

D	29	33	39	39	49
T	49.7	49.8	49.9	50.1	50.2
S	−16.6	−14.4	− 9.2	− 2.0	2.8
F	33.0	35.4	40.7	48.0	53.0
FE	− 4.0	− 2.4	− 1.7	− 9.0	− 4.0

Table 12.7   *Seasonal and residual factors in an additive model*

1971	J	F	M	A	M	J	J	A	S	O	N	D
D						60.0	65.0	67.0	63.0	50.0	35.0	30.0
T						46.9	46.9	46.9	46.9	46.9	46.9	46.9
D–T						13.1	18.1	20.1	16.1	3.1	−11.9	−16.9
S						11.4	17.8	19.8	16.8	3.1	−10.9	−16.9
R						1.7	0.3	0.3	− 0.7	0.0	− 1.0	0.0
1972												
D	29.0	30.0	36.0	44.0	51.0	59.0	65.0	66.0	65.0	50.0	36.0	30.0
T	46.9	46.9	46.9	46.9	46.9	46.9	46.9	46.9	46.9	46.9	46.9	46.9
D–T	−17.9	−16.9	−10.9	− 2.9	4.1	12.1	18.1	19.1	18.1	3.1	−10.9	−16.9
S	−17.2	−14.9	− 9.6	− 2.2	2.8	11.4	17.8	19.8	16.8	3.1	−10.9	−16.9
R	− 0.7	− 2.0	− 1.3	− 0.7	1.3	0.7	0.3	− 0.7	1.3	0.0	0.0	0.0
1973												
D	31.0	34.0	38.0	44.0	49.0	56.0	64.0	67.0	63.0	50.0	37.0	30.0
T	46.9	46.9	46.9	46.9	46.9	46.9	46.9	46.9	46.9	46.9	46.9	46.9
D–T	−15.9	−12.9	− 8.9	− 2.9	2.1	9.1	17.1	20.1	16.1	3.1	− 9.9	−16.9
S	−17.2	−14.9	− 9.6	− 2.2	2.8	11.4	17.8	19.8	16.8	3.1	−10.9	−16.9
R	1.3	2.0	0.7	− 0.7	− 0.7	− 2.3	− 0.7	0.3	− 0.7	0.0	1.0	0.0

1974

D	29.0	32.0	38.0	46.0	49.0	57.0	66.0	72.0	66.0	49.0	36.0	30.0
T	46.9	46.9	46.9	46.9	46.9	46.9	46.9	46.9	46.9	46.9	46.9	46.9
D–T	−17.9	−14.9	− 8.9	− 0.9	2.1	11.4	17.8	19.8	16.8	3.1	−10.9	−16.9
S	−17.2	−14.9	− 9.6	− 2.2	2.8							
R	− 0.7	0.0	0.7	1.3	− 0.7							
F						58.3	64.7	66.7	63.7	50.0	36.0	30.0
FE						− 1.3	1.3	5.3	2.3	− 1.0	0.0	0.0

1975

D	29.0	33.0	39.0	39.0	49.0
T	46.9	46.9	46.9	46.9	46.9
S	−17.2	−14.9	− 9.6	− 2.2	− 2.8
F	29.7	32.0	37.3	44.7	49.7
FE	− 0.7	1.0	1.7	− 5.7	− 0.7

from each season; if the error is negative, it is added. This forces the sum of the seasonal factors to equal zero.

Subtracting the seasonal factors from the de-trended series leaves the residual (or unexplained) variation. If the model works well then the residual values will be small relative to the original data. Table 12.6 presents the residual series.

An examination of Table 12.6 (and of Figure 12.3(b) which is based upon it) reveals a serious problem, namely that there is a trend in the residuals. These should be randomly distributed. If they are not then some information within the data set is not being captured by the model and the model is said to be mis-specified. Here the problem arises from the fact that the regression trend line is not significant – in particular, the slope coefficient is not significantly different from zero. The value calculated by the regression may simply be due to chance. The results presented in Table 12.6 tend to confirm that this is the case. It is possible that the lack of a time trend is because some kind of seasonal smoothing has already been applied to the data, although this is not mentioned in the data source.

In Table 12.6 the residuals show a clear downward trend. Two sets of data (June to December 1971, and January to May 1975) are available to test the forecasting ability of the model, since these periods were not used in its construction. Looking at the forecasts (F, calculated as $T+S$), and at the forecast error ($FE, = D-F$), we can see that the forecasts are all too low in the earlier period and too high in the later one (Figure 12.3(a)). This pattern in the forecast errors also arises from the mis-specification of the model.

If there is no trend in the data set, then the best which can be done is to calculate the mean value of the series. The spread of values around this mean is due to seasonal and random factors.

Since we no longer need to use complete years to estimate the trend, we can use the first 36 months' data to establish the model, and the final 12 to test it. This is the more usual approach. The mean occupancy level calculated over the first 36 months is 46.9%. In Table 12.7, this value is taken as the trend value and is subtracted from the observed data to give a de-trended set. The seasonal factors, residuals and forecasts are then calculated in exactly the same manner as above and are also included in Table 12.7.

Table 12.7 shows a much more satisfactory set of results. As is apparent from figure 12.3(c) and (d), there is no obvious pattern in the residuals, which seem to be randomly distributed. The F and FE values calculated for June 1974 onwards are calculated as before. The model performs creditably; for the most part, the forecast errors are small.

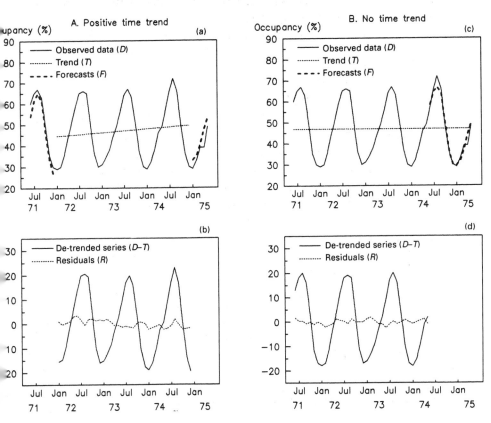

Figure 12.3 *Additive seasonal data analysis –
hotel occupancy in Great Britain (1971–5)*

A multiplicative model

The multiplicative model is best applied in situations where there is a
marked trend. Here we apply the general model:

$$D = T \times S \times C \times R$$

Once again, let us consider an example. Table 12.8 presents an index of
weekly turnover in UK catering establishments over the period 1969 to
1975. The data are quarterly – i.e. they represent an average week for each
quarter.

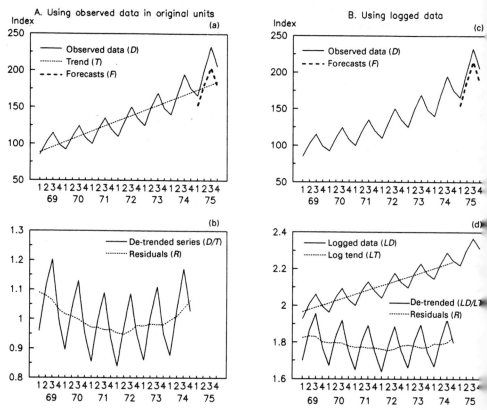

Figure 12.4 *Multiplicative seasonal data analysis – index of turnover per week in British catering (1969–75)*

Table 12.8 *An index of weekly turnover in UK catering establishments*

Quarter Year	1	2	3	4
1969	85	102	115	99
1970	92	110	124	108
1971	100	120	135	119
1972	110	131	150	134
1973	125	150	169	148
1974	140	169	195	175
1975	166	201	233	206

Source: Medlik and Airey (1978, Table 71, pp. 236–237)

Table 12.8 presents the results of an analysis based on a linear trend. The trend line based on the period 1969:1 to 1974:4 and estimated using linear regression is:

$$T = 85.03261 + 3.54739 \times QUARTER$$

| (t-values) | (15.000) | (8.942) | $r^2 = 0.78421$ |

As we can see from the t-values and r^2, and also from Figure 12.4(a), this equation provides a relatively good fit to the data. As before the final year is not used in trend estimation, being kept instead for use as a control on forecasting ability.

Trend values are calculated for each quarter (Table 12.9) and are then used to establish a de-trended series. In this case, we have:

$$D = T \times S \times R$$

dividing D by T therefore leaves a combination of seasonal and random factors:

$$D/T = S \times R$$

The values of D/T are then summed for each of the four quarters and divided by 6 (years 1969 to 1974). This gives the seasonal factor. We then divide the de-trended series by these seasonal factors leaving the residuals. Once again the important point is that if the model is correctly specified, there should be no pattern in the residuals.

A glance at Figure 12.4(b) shows that the residuals display a strong U-shaped pattern, indicating that the model is mis-specified. As a result, the forecasts are not very accurate.

In this case there is no simple solution to the problem. We cannot merely ignore the time trend as we did with the additive model since it is clearly significant. Looking at the observed data set in Figure 12.4(a), the trend line which would seem best to fit the data is an upward-sloping curve. Mathematically, this kind of relationship is often well estimated by taking logs of the original data. Other transformations of the data could also be tried – for example, given the shape of the residuals curve, it might be useful to square root the observed data before analysing it.

In the section that follows, we will use a log transformation of the data. The basic method of analysis remains exactly the same. We begin by taking logs of each data point giving a new series (LD), presented in Table 12.10 and Figure 12.4(c). Using this series, we calculate a time trend using regression. The equation of this trend is:

$$LT= \quad 1.95453 \quad + \quad 0.01181 \quad \times QUARTER$$

(*t*-values) (108.493) (9.366) $\qquad r^2 = 0.79951$

We then calculate the de-trended series of the log data (*LD/LT*). The seasonal factors and the residuals are calculated as before. Plotting the values of *R* we can see (Figure 12.4(d)) that there remains a U-shaped pattern, although this is much less marked than in the previous case. As a result, the forecasts are improved; the forecast errors being less than before.

Forecast values are calculated as follows. For each quarter, we calculate the log trend value and multiply it by the appropriate seasonal factor. For quarter 1 of 1975, the log trend is 2.24978 and the seasonal factor is 0.973776. The result (2.190781) is a forecast of turnover in log form. To get this back into the original units, we calculate 10 to the power of 2.190781 (which is 155.2). Note this assumes we are using logs to base 10. If another base, such as e, is used then this value replaces 10 in the calculations.

Discussion

The two examples developed are illustrative of the possibilities of time-series data analysis. Using fairly simple methods, quite reasonable results may be obtained. In many situations, fairly reliable forecasts are not too difficult to generate. Where the above methods fail, more sophist-icated techniques may work. A discussion of these techniques is beyond the scope of this text. The interested reader is referred to Makridakis *et al* (1983).

The examples also reveal, however, the Achilles' heel of time-series modelling. In the additive model, the forecasts for August 1974 and April 1975 are both in error by over 5 percentage points. In the multiplicative model, all four forecasts understate what in fact occurred. In both cases, the drawback is that we have no way within the model of explaining what has happened. This is because we are merely analysing past data and looking for patterns. We hope that these patterns will continue into the future and we base our forecasts upon them.

A different approach is offered by econometrics. Rather than simply pushing past data into the future, an attempt is made to identify important independent variables and to estimate their impact on the dependent variable. For instance, the example at the beginning of this chapter related occupancy (the dependent variable) to price (the inde-pendent variable). Although a relationship was found between the two,

Table 12.9 *The calculation of seasonal factors, residuals and forecasts in a multiplicative model*

Quarter Year	1	2	3	4
1969	85	102	115	99
T	88.580000	92.127390	95.674780	99.222170
D/T	0.959585	1.107163	1.201989	0.997761
S	0.881031	1.025663	1.130488	0.967485
R	1.089161	1.079460	1.063248	1.031293
1970	92	110	124	108
T	102.769560	106.316950	109.864340	113.411730
D/T	0.895207	1.034642	1.128665	0.952282
S	0.881031	1.025663	1.130488	0.967485
R	1.016090	1.008755	0.998388	0.984286
1971	100	120	135	119
T	116.959120	120.506510	124.053900	127.601290
D/T	0.855000	0.995797	1.088237	0.932592
S	0.881031	1.025663	1.130488	0.967485
R	0.970453	0.970881	0.962626	0.963935
1972	110	131	150	134
T	131.148680	134.696070	138.243460	141.790850
D/T	0.838743	0.972560	1.085042	0.945054
S	0.881031	1.025663	1.130488	0.967485
R	0.952001	0.948226	0.959800	0.976815
1973	125	150	169	148
T	145.338240	148.885630	152.433020	155.980410
D/T	0.860063	1.007485	1.108684	0.948837
S	0.881031	1.025663	1.130488	0.967485
R	0.976200	0.982277	0.980713	0.980725
1974	140	169	195	175
T	159.527800	163.075190	166.622580	170.169970
D/T	0.877590	1.036332	1.170310	1.028384
S	0.881031	1.025663	1.130488	0.967485
R	0.996094	1.010402	1.035225	1.062945
1975	166	201	233	206
T	173.717360	177.264750	180.812140	184.359530
S	0.881031	1.025663	1.130488	0.967485
F	153.1	181.8	204.4	178.4
FE	12.9	19.2	28.6	27.6

Table 12.10   *Seasonal analysis and forecasting of turnover per week (observed data in logs of original units)*

Quarter Year	1	2	3	4
1969	85	102	115	99
LD	1.929419	2.008600	2.060698	1.995635
LT	1.966340	1.978150	1.989960	2.001770
LD/LT	0.981223	1.015393	1.035547	0.996935
S	0.973776	1.005914	1.026194	0.994122
R	1.007648	1.009423	1.009115	1.002830
1970	92	110	124	108
LD	1.963788	2.041393	2.093422	2.033424
LT	2.013580	2.025390	2.037200	2.049010
LD/LT	0.975272	1.007901	1.027598	0.992393
S	0.973776	1.005914	1.026194	0.994122
R	1.001536	1.001975	1.001368	0.998261
1971	100	120	135	119
LD	2.000000	2.079181	2.130334	2.075547
LT	2.060820	2.072630	2.084440	2.096250
LD/LT	0.970487	1.003161	1.022017	0.990124
S	0.973776	1.005914	1.026194	0.994122
R	0.996623	0.997263	0.995930	0.995979
1972	110	131	150	134
LD	2.041393	2.117271	2.176091	2.127105
LT	2.108060	2.119870	2.131680	2.143490
LD/LT	0.968375	0.998774	1.020834	0.992356
S	0.973776	1.005914	1.026194	0.994122
R	0.994454	0.992902	0.994777	0.998224
1973	125	150	169	148
LD	2.096910	2.176091	2.227887	2.170262
LT	2.155300	2.167110	2.178920	2.190730
LD/LT	0.972909	1.004144	1.022473	0.990657
S	0.973776	1.005914	1.026194	0.994122
R	0.999110	0.998240	0.996374	0.996515
1974	140	169	195	175
LD	2.146128	2.227887	2.290035	2.243038
LT	2.202540	2.214350	2.226160	2.237970
LD/LT	0.974388	1.006113	1.028693	1.002265
S	0.973776	1.005914	1.026194	0.994122
R	1.000629	1.000198	1.002435	1.008191
1975	166	201	233	206
LT	2.249780	2.261590	2.273400	2.285210
S	0.973776	1.005914	1.026194	0.994122
LF	2.190781	2.274966	2.332949	2.271777
F	155.2	188.4	215.3	187.0
FE	10.8	12.6	17.7	19.0

we concluded that other independent variables must also be playing a role in the determination of occupancy levels. Such variables might include an index of exchange rates, consumer income, competitors prices, an index of room supply, and so on.

The econometric approach is to include all these elements within the same model. Regression techniques may then be applied to estimate the model. A number of such methods are available. Their derivation is somewhat more complex than the methods presented here. The interested reader is referred to the books by Thomas (1985) and Koutsoyiannis (1977), both of which are excellent introductions to econometrics. The application of the methods tends to be relatively straightforward since many computer software packages exist which estimate econometric models. The main difficulty is then one of interpretation of results and deciding when a 'good' model has been identified. Unless the user has some understanding of econometric principles, such decisions will be difficult to make.

Although econometric methods tend to be more difficult than time-series analysis, the advantage is that, as the dependent variable is related directly to some independent variables, forecasting errors can more easily be ascribed to their causes. The errors themselves may not be all that different between the two approaches, which leads some people to argue that the simpler approach should be used. Where the model is being used on a one-off basis, this may be a valid argument. If, however, there is an attempt to provide forecasts on an ongoing basis, it would seem difficult to improve the model if we cannot identify why it is going wrong. Once again, the correct choice of model will depend on the use to which it is to be put.

In the case of the two examples developed above, only *ad-hoc* explanations can be put forward. The cause of the unusual occupancy results can only be guessed at – perhaps exchange rate movements or the weather. In the case of turnover, the explanation of the forecasting errors seems clearer. During the early 1970s, inflation accelerated in the UK, exceeding 25% in 1975. Since the data have not been adjusted for inflation, it is the acceleration in this which explains the underestimate in forecast values. An obvious approach, and one that is frequently used, would be to deflate the turnover index using the retail price index. We would then forecast turnover volume. However, if we are interested in forecasting turnover value, then we do not get very far since we now have the problem of forecasting inflation. Such forecasts are regularly provided by the government and also by various economic forecasters. It is left as an exercise for the interested reader to look at the accuracy of such forecasts over, say, a one-month and a one-year period ahead.

Conclusion

This chapter has introduced a variety of topics important to the analysis of time-series data. Index numbers are widely used for the presentation of such data and the principal methods used for their calculation were considered. Frequently data are available on a number of variables and it is of interest to investigate the relationships which might exist between them. The techniques of correlation and regression are the standard methods used for such investigations. Finally, the forecasting of time-series data is essential for a variety of management decisions. Such forecasts may be arrived at using many different methods. This chapter has looked at the application of one particular method and considered the general problem of how to evaluate the accuracy of the forecasts obtained. The interested reader cannot be encouraged too strongly to follow up the references given below.

References

MAKRIDAKIS, S., WHEELWRIGHT, S. and McGEE, V. (1983), *Forecasting: Methods and Applications*, 2nd edn, John Wiley, New York.

THOMAS, R. (1985), *Introductory Econometrics*, Longman.

KOUTSOYIANNIS, A. (1977), *Theory of Econometrics*, 2nd edn, Macmillan.

For an application of some of the ideas discussed in this chapter see:

ARBEL, A. (1983),'Higher energy costs and the demand for restaurant services – a time series analysis', *International Journal of Hospitality Management*, **2(2)**: 83–87.

FERGUSON, D. and SELLING, T. (1983), 'Analyzing food and labour costs', *Cornell HRA Quarterly*, November, pp. 31–39.

HARRIS, P. (1986), 'The application of regression and correlation techniques for cost planning and control decisions in the hotel industry', *International Journal of Hospitality Management*, **5(3)**: 127–133.

LEE, D. (1984), 'A forecast of lodging supply and demand', *Cornell HRA Quarterly*, August, pp. 27–40.

See also the interesting series of articles entitled 'Getting the most from marketing research' by Lewis, R. which appeared in the *Cornell HRA Quarterly* in 6 parts – November 1983 pp. 81–85; February 1984 pp. 25–35; May 1984 pp. 54–69; November 1984 pp. 64–77; February 1985 pp. 82–96 and August 1985 pp. 86–99. This series of articles makes use of many of the techniques discussed throughout this book (and one or two others besides).

Exercises

1 Obtain data for the food-cost index over, say, the past five years.
   (a) What kind of index is this?
   (b) What weights are used and how are they determined?
2 *Lloyds Bank Economic Bulletin* for September 1980 gives the following
   information regarding tourist spending and exchange rates (the data
   set is presented graphically in Chapter 2).

Year	Tourist spending	£/....change rate
1972	1.6	2.48
1973	1.9	2.44
1974	1.9	2.36
1975	2.2	2.22
1976	2.7	1.80
1977	3.2	1.78
1978	3.0	1.92
1979	2.8	2.12
1980	2.6	2.30

   (a) Calculate the sample correlation coefficient.
   (b) Calculate the least squares regression line.
   (c) Interpret your results.
3 Construct an additive and a multiplicative model of public house
   turnover over a 7-year period using either the data for 1969 to 1975
   Medlik and Airey pp. 236–7, or using more recent data from Business
   Monitor.

Index

def – p. 144